THE INTERNET'S F1RST ENTREPRENEUR

ALSO BY ALAN MARSHALL MECKLER

The Draft and Its Enemies: A Documentary History,
University Of Illinois Press, 1974 (*with* John J. O'sullivan)

Oral History Collections, R.R. Bowker, 1975 (*with* Ruth Mcmullen)

Micropublishing: A History of Scholarly Micropublishing
in America, 1938-1980, Greenwood Press, 1982

The Complete Guide to Playing Lotteries by Mail, Dell, 1985

THE INTERNET'S F1RST ENTREPRENEUR

LESSONS AND WISDOM FOR THE BUSINESS JOURNEY

ALAN MARSHALL MECKLER

/l|BookBaby Publishing

ISBN: 978-1-66780-069-1 (hardcover)
ISBN: 978-1-66780-070-7 (eBook)

To Ellen Laurie, who continues by my side
with all the ups and downs, ne plus ultra

And the best kind of client? The first generation entrepreneur, hands-down…there's not one of them who has not had a close brush with commercial oblivion. They know how to turn adversity into opportunity. They can see that a bear market is really a kind of value-restoration event. Or they can summon the courage to try again when they really do go for broke. They remember the people who stood by them, and they remember the ones who didn't.

—James Grant
Grant's Interest Rate Observer

CONTENTS

ACKNOWLEDGEMENT

I want to thank Ellis Booker for help with editing this book over a three-year period. In 1995, Ellis was part of the founding staff of *Web Week*, our first weekly, news-oriented offering aimed at internet professionals; later, after joining CMP, he competed with my publications. He has been an invaluable helper. I also had significant help from Tony Abbott, who worked for me many years ago as editor in chief (1979-1995). Tony today is a noted author of novels for teens and more. And thanks to so many incredible colleagues who worked with me from 1971 through today. None of my accomplishments could have occurred without yeoman service from all of you.

INTRODUCTION

It is December 1996. I am in a sort of "crow's nest" at the Javits Convention Center in New York City. The view is incredible. I am positioned so I can look over the expanse of the convention center, the size of several square city blocks. I can see perhaps 500 tech company displays, some as large as 10,000 square feet. At any given time, there are 20,000 or more people milling about, ambling along or darting in and out of the vendor booths, which include the likes of Microsoft, Hewlett-Packard, IBM and a myriad of others. Along with these tech giants are dozens of startups that have launched in the dawn of the Internet Revolution, which is a mere two years old.

I am awestruck! I am the creator of this colossus. The show will make my company, Mecklermedia, several million dollars. Only three years earlier, I was close to personal bankruptcy, living on a home equity line of credit and 20 credit cards, and not knowing from one month to the next if I could make payroll for my company of 10 employees. I have to pinch myself to make sure this is not a dream.

I had embarked on being an entrepreneur 25 years earlier, producing a publication for research libraries out of my home in Weston, Connecticut. In between, I had four children with my wife, started numerous publications, databases, events and more. Most of these efforts had some critical success, but nothing of note financially. But I kept at it, with idea after idea. My own family told me that I was a ne'er-do-well or just a dreamer, with nothing to show for years and years of hard work. Often short of operating funds, my efforts to raise money for my various ideas hadn't had positive results. Many prospective investors responded to my ideas with scorn or ridicule. On a personal level, I was dyslexic who faced incredible hurdles all along the way.

But on that December day in 1996, as I watched over my Internet World colossus, I smiled. I was a 51-year-old who had finally achieved world-class critical and financial success, 25 years after embarking on an entrepreneurial life. It was difficult to think it was real (little did I know that I would reach even greater success in the coming years). It would never be a perfectly smooth road, nor would I always choose the correct fork when confronted with major decisions and opportunities.

I hope readers will use this memoir as an encouragement, as an example that one should never give up the dream, and that success can happen to anyone who has the courage to be an entrepreneur.

EARLY LIFE, PERSONAL LIFE & FEELINGS

50 YEARS AN ENTREPRENEUR

I have been an entrepreneur for over 50 years. Even as a young boy, I had ideas for business startups. As a 10-year-old, I wrote to the Spaulding sporting goods company to suggest that they sell football helmets for every professional team, with each team's logo on the helmet. In those days (1955) there were about a dozen teams in the NFL, and only the Baltimore Colts and the Los Angeles Rams had logos on the sides of their respective helmets. The response from Spaulding was a threat of legal action if I decided to pursue my concept.

This was the first of many turndowns that I have received in my career. I was not deterred. I soon came up with the idea that Pepsi Cola should introduce the concept of Pepsi ice popsicles. Pepsi's response was kinder. I received a very nice letter from a corporate vice president telling me that Pepsi appreciated my idea but that they had already contemplated such a product and had rejected it.

My father was an entrepreneur, credited with inventing the concept of leasing fleet vehicles back in the 1940s. He built a significant business through the 1960s, marked by ingenuity around making acquisitions and evolving his businesses with new concepts. I soaked up his conversations with his business associates and became fascinated with new business ideas. My father never went out of his way to include me in meetings, but he was 24/7 business, and so dinner time conversation, when he was present, was usually devoted to stories about deals and personalities. I realize now that I formed opinions about men and women who worked for my father, even though I had never met them. Along with numerous successes, there were disappointments for my father along the way, and in the end he suffered bankruptcy. This was a lesson too.

By the age of 20 I had witnessed his elation and his depression. Watching these trials and tribulations prepared me for my own endeavors and ups and downs. Looking back, I realize that there are few people like Bill Gates, people who had one idea that they developed and reached a huge success overnight. Most successful entrepreneurs have made several launches, and have had many disasters along the way to a final success. In 1994, I was interviewed by a writer for Forbes after my company, Mecklermedia, had its initial public offering. I was 49 years old at the time. I remember being asked what took me so long to be successful. My answer was related to my love of baseball, as I believe baseball offers life lessons on both failure and success. I said that a .300 hitter in baseball would be elected to the Baseball Hall of Fame, but such stats meant the person failed to be successful 70 percent of the time. "My mentality was like a baseball hitter," he quotes me saying. "If you can be successful three times out of ten, you're phenomenal." But the writer decided to be nasty, concluding in his article that one should be careful about investing in Mecklermedia because, while .300 was a great percentage in baseball, it meant that more times than not the hitter was unsuccessful. "MecklerWeb," he wrote, "alas, may end up like many of his other projects: a good idea but not a good profit maker."

The interview was a punch to the gut; I felt I had been sucker punched by the writer. Perhaps his immigrant background prevented him from understanding baseball, but my feeling to this day was that he was nasty, turning an interesting story into an attack because he did not believe in the future of the fledgling Internet (a Mecklermedia stock purchaser in 1994 would have made 10x on the investment by 1998).

By the time of the aforementioned *Forbes* article, a good guesstimate is that I had started or tried to start several hundred specialty tech, scholarly, or consumer publications, ranging in topics as diverse as baseball, botany, white-collar crime, recorded books, old wooden boats, CD-ROM and, of course, the Internet. In addition, by 1994, I had made at least 50 attempts in the conference/trade show business. I simply could not pass up what I deemed a good idea, and was always convincing myself that the next launch would deliver incredible financial returns. Interestingly, almost every endeavor garnered critical success. But I learned, over and over again, that while it is nice to have critical success, such accolades do not pay the bills, particularly when one has, as I had by this time, a wife and four children to support.

This book backs up my claim that I was the first person to start a commercial business related to the Internet. That business was an academic newsletter called Research and Education Networking, that launched in October 1990, or more than three years before The World Wide Web became commercially known in December 1993. It may be hard to fathom today, but the commercial possibility of the internet was only vaguely understood at the time. John Markoff of *The New York Times* wrote a front-page article about the World Wide Web in the first week of December 1993.

I chose this title because few people in the academic or business world knew the term "Internet." In mid-1993, I changed the name to Internet World and broadened the coverage to include Internet business applications at the suggestion of the founder of Lotus, Mitch Kapor, who agreed to be a keynote speaker for me at a forerunner to my Internet World trade show in January 1992 in New York City. My losses were quite large trying to get this publication off the ground, and I considered ceasing publication several times through 1992.

This book covers 50 years of memories and lessons learned from my experiences, and spends a good deal of time discussing the early days of the commercial Internet and some of the people who were true pioneers. Looking back from 30 years, it is shocking to me how many so-called tech and media movers and shakers were not only Internet doubters, but would not give me the time of day to discuss the investment opportunity I offered. In part this reluctance had to do with my record up until 1993, which was one of no single success in content publishing. I suppose I was looked at as a nice guy with lots of interests, but, at 49 years of age, a business failure.

The economist and author Nassim Talib, in his book *Black Swan* (2007), speculates that there might be at most one or two black swan events per century. The black swan theory states that until explorers found black swans in Australia in 1697, there was certainty that *all* swans were white. Thus, a black swan event is essentially a world-shattering occurrence that totally changes the thoughts of mankind and is revolutionary. I would suggest that while I did not create the Internet, I was the first, or among the first, pioneer to see its commercial possibilities. Vinton Cerf and other scientists had, long before me, seen the Internet as a breakthrough method for delivering information in times of possible calamity, such as nuclear war. But in all the years these scientists worked on building the Internet's backbone, neither they nor anybody else started commercial ventures. I would suggest that all my failed probes into new ventures, conferences and publications were the precursor to my finally hitting on a black swan event and an Internet fortune. And along the way, I learned many lessons, which are imparted in this book.

These experiences epitomize my career in that I have had many more failures than successes, or ideas that were both critically and financially successful. What are the ingredients needed to be critically and financially successful?

This book will convey a few cardinal rules, based on my experiences in life and in business. Many of these rules were painfully learned. The pain, oftentimes, was emotionally wrenching. But the elation that came with critical and financial success was indescribable.

There are several keywords that best describe my makeup as an entrepreneur: awareness, curious, optimistic, adaptable, paranoid and loyal. Let me briefly go over each of these traits.

Awareness is necessary to be an entrepreneur, although I do not believe it can be learned. It is part of daily life, similar to breathing. You cannot train yourself to be aware. There are different types of awareness, for sure. A combat soldier or a policeman in a dangerous situation is acutely aware. But in everyday life, awareness is observing while walking down the street or during daily reading, and then relating a visual or mental thought into an idea. In my case, awareness and interesting ideas come into my mind with motion (walking and driving) or during good conversation. My mind is always exploring.

When I was in grade school, teachers felt I was a lazy daydreamer who could not concentrate. But I remember that I was thinking *too much*, and thus their interpretation that I could not focus.

Being *curious* is related to being aware. I loved history and obtained a doctorate in American history. My love of history is related to being curious about why a certain figure made such and such a decision, or why an event caused the creation of an invention or a creative action. Every entrepreneur, even if unfamous, was sparked by being curious and aware, and thus develop an idea into a product or business. Like awareness, curiosity cannot be learned. One has it or does not. This does not mean that if one is not aware or curious he or she cannot be an entrepreneur. But it is more likely that an entrepreneur has one or both of these traits in abundance.

Optimism is another helpful trait for the entrepreneur. Many have said that I am eternally optimistic to a fault. It is helpful to be optimistic because failure is always around the corner. A person who is pessimistic is not likely to be an entrepreneur. A startup is fraught with danger around every corner. The optimist says, "Things will work out" or "The next investor is sure to come with the next pitch" or "The next design will clearly be a winner." If one is too realistic, it is unlikely the entrepreneur's path is for you.

Adaptability is so very important. One has to be able to adapt, since the path to success as an entrepreneur is not a straight one. Either the original concept fails, or an investor does not come through, or the competition surprises you. These and many other pitfalls are always around the corner. There are always what I call "forks in the road," as well as where a key decision has to be made—go left or go right. The wrong turn can lead to crisis, so adaptability is life and death for the startup. Sometimes one can recover, but it often means the end of the startup.

This is where being *optimistic* is helpful, even if it means starting all over again with another idea. It also means having to accept criticism or "taking arrows in the back," as failure brings out the naysayers. Are you able to come back from such events? Are you able to handle rejection from an investor pitch?

Paranoia is another trait that is important. My greatest weakness is being too loyal and not paranoid enough in my dealings with investors, employees and perceived friends. I lost a lot of money by staying too long with an employee out of loyalty, or thinking that an investor or individual, met through the course of business, was a loyal friend. It is disappointing to have to write this, but when one makes significant money, many people appear to become friends. But I have learned that they are of the fair weather variety. The change can be overnight. One day a friend, the next day not. This is a particularly painful experience. Fortunately, this area is not key to the making of an entrepreneur, but it is part of the whole experience.

An entrepreneur is in an exclusive class, as most people lack the innate traits necessary to become part of the class. The mix of pain and elation one has as an entrepreneur is often unbearable. I have never needed drugs or alcohol to handle the ups and downs of my life-long trek, but sometimes I have wondered why I put up with the pain. However, the highs that come with entrepreneurial success surely overcome the lows. I imagine that, like childbirth, one forgets the pain of the experience and goes for the joy, again and again.

In conclusion, let me turn to the baseball analogy that the Forbes writer turned against me many years ago. I am, at best, a .400 hitter when it comes to business ideas. Fortunately, while more of my startups have failed, those that succeeded were big winners. Hopefully, my ups and downs and wounds will inspire a new class of entrepreneurs to be emboldened and push ahead with their ideas. There is no drug better than taking an idea and making it a critical and financial success.

INCREDIBLE DISAPPOINTMENT

There are few things more depressing to an entrepreneur than thinking you are about to close a deal that will make you a nice return, only to learn in the 11th hour that the buyer has backed out. Unfortunately, I have had several of these encounters. It is hard to describe the shock, pain, depression and worse that can set in when something like this happens. I have always been an optimist, but at the same time I am certainly manic-depressive. Even in the leanest times, while I was building a business, I always felt I would be successful. Success to me had to be defined by a sale.

In my early days, when I created Microform Review in the 1970s, I thought a sale price of $100,000 marked a great success. However, by the time I sold this publication and its related properties in 1990 for $1 million to Klaus Saur, I had no feeling of accomplishment. That's because I needed the sale to buy out my Swedish partner, who thought I was dishonest. The sale was a means for me to concentrate on new things — the Internet, CD-ROM and Virtual Reality — and none of the funds hit my pocket.

The closest I came to elation was in 1992, when a trade show group in England by the name Blenheim offered me $1.5 million for a trade show I had created three years earlier called Optical Information Systems. With the deal all but completed, I went out and bought a new suit and some clothes for the first time in many years. But on the morning of the closing, the Blenheim team pulled the plug on the deal. What was worse: the deal would have relieved me of some debt and given me breathing room to develop other properties. Unfortunately, Blenheim decided that they could engage a key consultant I had been using in England and start a competing show that could be successful for a lot less than $1.5 million.

Objectively, Blenheim made a good move, as with their deeper pockets they would have destroyed my show. (In fact, my show eventually failed, as did theirs.)

The level of depression that sets in after deal failure depends, of course, on how much one "needs" the deal. The Blenheim deal was badly needed. I remember functioning, but being in a fog or daze as I went about my business and family life. It is a horrible state of mind and numbing.

My ability to look for options and be resilient in hard times came through, and I realized I had to get something done.

I got in touch with Steve Monnington, the lead business development person at Blenheim, and arranged a meeting at their headquarters in London, England. I flew overnight and appeared at the Blenheim offices at 9 a.m. With my heart on my sleeve, I told Monnington that the deal failure would put me out of business. Was there any way they would pay me for my mailing lists, other records and branding? I asked for $100,000. After a bit of thought, the deal was done and I walked out with a check on the spot for $75,000. The money was a company-saver for me. I took a big gamble that Blenheim would go for my proposal, as they would remove me as a competitor and gain mailing list and trademark assets. Monnington was only out of the room for 15 minutes, so it proved to be a good deal for Blenheim. I went from getting $1.5 million to $75,000 in a few days. Shocking, but it enabled me to stay in business.

MORE INCREDIBLE DISAPPOINTMENT

I had a series of major disappointments in my dealing with Jonathan Klein, CEO and co-founder of Getty Images from 2006 to 2008. I mentioned earlier how I entered the online stock photo business in 2003. From 2003 until well into 2006, my company was a Wall Street darling, and the market cap of our public stock grew from several million dollars to $700 million. Corbis, owned by Microsoft's Bill Gates but operated by others, tried to buy our Jupiterimages several times during this period.

Looking back, one of my greatest mistakes was listening to my board and lieutenants and not selling to Corbis, who approached us three different times. The other suitor was Jonathan Klein of Getty Images. Klein, along with Mark Getty, had created Getty Images in the late 1990s. The company was the goliath of the stock photo business; it was a veritable cash-flow machine. After turning down Corbis several times, I started getting deal offers from Klein.

Eventually, in 2007, Getty offered to buy all of our image assets for $370 million in cash. The deal had several ups and downs for a variety of reasons that have been described elsewhere. Nevertheless, Klein was "hot to trot" and seemed to be salivating to make the deal. Everything was in place for an early morning closing in March 2007. The night before the signing, all last-minute wrinkles had been smoothed out and we were ready to go. Then, at 6:30 a.m., I got a call from my lead attorney saying that he had received an email and a call from the Getty attorney that they had decided to walk away from the deal.

Even though by this time in my career I was financially well-off, the Getty pull-back was mentally draining and debilitating to me for many weeks. Even as I write this in 2021, I can still feel the shock and numbness about the deal not taking place. It is nearly impossible for any reader to understand such feelings, unless they've experienced a similar event. I have always been good at recuperating from these kinds of shocks, but this event took its toll.

Why didn't the Getty deal close? I believe it was because of a particular Getty board member's negative feelings about me, because of something I had written about him years earlier. Klein never confirmed this, and never gave me a reason for his pulling out.

CHINA, 1999-2001

My memories of China in the late 1990s are amazing, when you think about China today. For example, my guide, who was about 50 years old, had just bought a mobile phone, after having been on a waiting list for more than 20 years to get a landline. I remember him telling me that in China many transactions were already on mobile phones. As we know, this means of conducting business in China has only grown, and now far surpasses what we have the U.S. While most of the cars were rickety and not Western brands, the "in" car in those days was the American Buick. For some reason, the Buick meant status. The St. Regis where I was staying had a small fleet of black Buicks to take guests to the airport and elsewhere. I have often wondered if the Chinese fascination with Buicks is what saved this brand when General Motors decided to cease making the Pontiac and Oldsmobile.

Most of all, I remember the hustle and enthusiasm of the Chinese entrepreneurs that I met with, and their excitement to show me their respective business plans. Unfortunately for me, I decided to invest in a few of the startups that did not produce good results. My mistake was believing in some of the expats who were partnered with these Chinese entrepreneurs. Later, I found out that several of these characters were less than honest. In one case, an email newsletter publisher seemed to be thriving, but as his business increased, the results seemed to go downhill. I later found out that he had set up several companies outside of China, and was moving the better assets into LLCs he'd set up in the Caymans and elsewhere so that I could not track these shenanigans.

It was also on this trip that one young Chinese fellow named John Liu appealed to me to become my "man in China." He wanted to set up a conference and news company based on my Internet.com, to report on Chinese Internet tech and software development. He had a job with Asian *Wall Street Journal,* and, in fact, Dow Jones, the owner of the paper at that time, was offering to send him to business school in the U.S. to get an MBA. I told him to take the business school offer, but in the end he really craved working for Internet.com, and so I hired him. And he was amazing. He set up an office for us and made some hires. We started a series of seminars, which were modestly successful. He even arranged for me to have lunch with all the CEOs of the startup search engine companies in Beijing on a subsequent trip to China. All was going well, but then the Internet crash in the spring of 2000 hit, and we had to close Beijing and several other overseas bureaus, including Singapore and Sydney. I was not able to keep track of John, but I presume that with his remarkable drive and connections, he is a successful fellow these days.

MY FIRST STARTUP

After spending six months in military basic training and active duty in the New York Air National Guard in 1969, my first two jobs were with two companies in the scholarly publishing arena. Even though I had no experience, I was hired by Cornell Jaray. Cornell had a specialty publishing company called Kennikat Press, based in Port Washington, New York. A true entrepreneur, Cornell had taken a rare book business and turned it into a specialty book publisher in an area called scholarly reprint publishing.

During the Great Society initiative under President Lyndon Johnson, huge amounts of money poured into the economy in the form of building community and junior colleges across the U.S. All of these new schools had new libraries that lacked books. The reprint business was born during this time to help stock these libraries with copies of books long out of print, but necessary as the cornerstone of a library collection.

Cornell, a rare book dealer, noticed that original copies of books, ones he might sell one or two copies a year, were now in demand; suddenly, he could sell hundreds of the same title. Within a few years, this small specialty segment of the book trade became hot. I was the first non-family hire at Kennikat, which had recently been acquired by INSILCO for a few million dollars. It was a time when large publishers and specialty conglomerates were busy buying reprint companies. *The New York Times* had acquired a competitor of Kennikat's called Arno Press; the august trade publisher Farrar, Straus and Giroux had acquired Octagon; Harcourt had acquired Johnson Reprint.

Cornell wanted to grow Kennikat because he had an earn-out from INSILCO that was based on growth and profits. Amazingly, I was hired to be the director of marketing. It was a fascinating time for me because I had to learn on the job. Jaray showed me the ropes, and I learned rapidly. I would write the promotional copy for the several hundred books we planned to publish in the coming year. Also, I was sent to the larger book publishing trade shows to man the Kennikat exhibit booth. These included the American Library Association's two annual trade shows, and others. I soaked this up and learned the trade show business as well as the publishing trade.

At one of these trade shows, I came across a competitor called Greenwood Press, based in Westport, Connecticut. After 15 months of hard work, I was recruited by Greenwood to be its marketing director at 25 years old. The Kennikat experience had been fabulous. I learned everything one could know about scholarly book marketing in less than two years and had leap-frogged over people years my senior because of my Kennikat training and deep immersion in the scholarly book trade. This included observing how trade shows operated, even though at the time I would not have speculated that this business would be where I would make my fortune.

As I have stated, the entrepreneur has to be aware and open to learning rapidly. Essentially, one has to be a pirate, ready to apply what has been learned on the next job or start-up. Some people are not geared to think in this manner. Back then, and even now, I tend to think outside the box. I was always ready to suggest new ways of marketing at Kennikat and at Greenwood, and mentally noting what was not working and what might work. I became frustrated by the pace of change and would suggest that most entrepreneurs grow frustrated working for someone else. The overwhelming majority of workers are pleased to have a job and hope for an annual raise. I, on the other hand, was constantly planning for my own publishing business. All I needed was a "vertical" idea that I could grab.

That idea arrived about one year after I joined Greenwood Press. Greenwood was another scholarly reprint publisher that was owned by a public company in the specialty paper business called Williamhouse-Regency. The founders of Greenwood, both named Harold, were in their 50s. Both had experience in book publishing: Harold Mason had been an antiquarian bookseller; his partner, Harold Schwartz, had been in various marketing positions. They joined together and convinced Williamhouse-Regency paper company to back their scholarly reprint venture. Growth at Greenwood was spectacular. The two Harolds were making a lot of money from stock options. Their deal was geared to revenue growth, so whatever could increase sales was pushed aggressively. When Greenwood pushed into publishing historical archives on microfiche and microfilm in 1971, they figured they had hit the "mother lode." Soon, they asked me to take over marketing these expensive collections, which included all the Congressional Hearings of the United States, a collection that they sold for $15,000.

I immediately delved into this arena and started a massive campaign with the larger research and public libraries in the U.S. The two Harolds told me that if I could sell 20 sets in one year, I would get a $5000 cash bonus (my salary at the time was $15,000). I embarked on a phone and letter campaign, but also visited a dozen institutions in the northeast in February 1971. It was during a drive between Dartmouth College in Hanover, New Hampshire, and Durham, New Hampshire, which was home to the University of New Hampshire, that the vertical idea I had been seeking popped into my head.

I realized that the librarians I met with were being asked to spend $15,000 based on promotional materials from Greenwood Press. Yet in every other area of publishing for libraries, there were several review publications that librarians could analyze for recommendations on buying what they needed. Voila! *Start a magazine for librarians that reviewed microfiche and microfilm publications.* It would follow what had been done for books, periodicals and films for years. I mapped out the whole operation during this drive and my ultimate drive back to Westport, Connecticut, a few days later.

I also realized I would need an editorial board to give the review publication gravitas, as well as an editor in chief with a good reputation. Within a week, I had put out feelers to my editorial board candidates and had engaged, on a freelance basis, the assistant director at the Stanford University Libraries, and a noted expert in micropublishing, named Allen Veaner, to be the editor in chief.

I was still working at Greenwood, where, in a three-month period, I sold 20 sets of the Congressional Hearing collection. I requested my $5000 bonus, but was told by the two Harolds that Greenwood was having a cash-flow problem and they had to hold off giving me my bonus until the summer. Hearing this news, I now had no loyalty to Greenwood and announced my departure. I cashed in a small life insurance policy that I had purchased a few years earlier, and used $10,000 to start my first company, which I named Microform Review, Inc. My first direct mail effort was immediately successful, generating over 1500 subscriptions at $20-a-year.

In a period of two years, I had learned the ins and outs of the scholarly publishing business, as well as how to create and send out direct mail. It was a form of graduate school education. I was fortunate that, with both jobs, I was given tasks to perform that were above my "pay-grade," so my on-the-job training was demanding, but fruitful. I was a pro marketer in the niche field of scholarly publishing and off to the races. All this could not have happened if I had not been aware, and consciously and subconsciously readying myself for a startup.

MILITARY BASIC TRAINING

At the time I flew from the old Floyd Bennett Field in Brooklyn, New York, in February 1969 to Lackland Air Force Base in San Antonio, Texas, I did not think that basic training was going to be a grand experience, full of lessons that would help me immensely as an entrepreneur and in overseeing several companies as CEO.

It was February 1969, the height of the Vietnam War. For someone born in1945, one expected to serve, or have to deal with, military service. The draft, via Selective Service, had been in place since the beginning of World War II, and as a young man you had to register at your community or local draft board upon turning 18. Everyone was expected to serve, in peacetime or wartime. I knew all of this way too well, as my senior thesis at Columbia College was on the history of conscription in the United States. The choices were these: volunteer, join the reserves or National Guard, or get an exemption from service. About one-third of all draft-age men served in Vietnam, another third got out of Vietnam by entering the reserves or National Guard, and the last third got medical or some other type of exemption.

I was no hero (I had high school classmates who were killed in Vietnam or who were prisoners of war). I ended up serving in both the Air National Guard and the Army Reserve, from 1969 to 1975. This entailed 6 months of basic training and active duty, and 6 years of serving one weekend every month, plus two weeks of summer training. For most of us, the weekends and summer camps were drudgery of the highest level. Basic training was no picnic, as the training was the same whether you were going to Vietnam or serving on weekends. Of course, if you were going to be what was known as a "weekend warrior," your basic training did not have the 24/7 dread of having to go to Vietnam. Little did I know that within 48 hours of landing at Lackland and being yelled at by my training sergeant, I would be placed in charge of 40 young men from around the United States. After the shaved head and being suited up in fatigues, all 40 of us were petrified and knew nothing about being an airman. All we knew was that Sargent David Mariano was mean and always seemed angry. I mean he was *fierce-mean*, with the ability to yell, scream, and curse non-stop.

What you have seen in the movies about basic training is all true. Two days into getting the routine from Mariano, he pulled me aside.

"Meckler, you are what we call the Dorm Chief. I usually pick someone who can beat the shit out of all 40 of you, but you look smart, you have a masters degree, and you are going to be in charge from the time I leave the base at 5 p.m. until I return at 8:30 a.m. the next day. Here is your badge."

He pinned a red square badge with the words "Dorm Chief" in white letters on my uniform, over my left breast pocket.

"By tomorrow, you will learn to march the flight [the term for the group of 40-airmen] and you will be responsible for having barracks in tip-top shape for a full inspection every day at 8 a.m."

Wow. I was one super nervous person after being hit with this responsibility. I knew nothing about marching people and nothing about anything that I was being assigned. On top of everything else, Mariano gave me a pad of forms and a special red pencil, which he told me always had to be in my right breast pocket. The pad contained demerit forms. If one of the airmen got out of line, I could issue a demerit. Two demerits in a week meant the airman would have to repeat a week of basic training, and nobody wanted that punishment. It was the equivalent of carrying a club. While some of my fellow airmen gave me trouble, they always knew that if they went too far, I could hand them a demerit. Fortunately, I never had to.

The leadership training I got from being Dorm Chief was priceless. The confidence I gained from marching 40 people to breakfast and dinner for 6 weeks was riveting. I must say, seeing 40 people marching, stopping, turning on one's commands is powerful and pleasing. But most of all, I learned about handling pressure. True, this was not combat pressure, and in the big picture of the Vietnam War, what I did was a zero. However, the training was like getting another university degree or carrying an extra major. When things were tight in startup mode or payroll mode or taking on business adversaries (of which I have had many), the Dorm Chief role in basic training was priceless. Nothing could ever top the pressure placed on me that night by Sergeant Mariano. And few accomplishments in my business life have come close to topping the proud feeling I had of becoming a successful and confident Dorm Chief.

BILLIONAIRE FEELING

Billionaire is not the end of the world, but touching that level from a base of being broke six years earlier is riveting. I remember hovering at a billionaire "paper" net worth and going to a meeting with a real estate billionaire in New York City in early 2000. This was a nice fellow, who inherited his money, but nonetheless was and is successful.

The meeting was set up because my friend wanted me to help him vet a startup real estate venture. I remember being late to the meeting and that he introduced me as follows: "Meet Alan Meckler, who has become a billionaire in a few months, whereas as our family required many decades to attain this level."

The introduction was shocking because, at that point in time, I had never been introduced in such a manner. It was nice to be in the club, so to speak. I have related how King Harris warned me to place a financial collar or hedge on my paper net worth a few weeks after this meeting with the real estate mogul. King's advice was the route Mark Cuban wisely took after selling his Broadcast.com to Yahoo on April 1, 1999 for $5.7 billion. Cuban saw Yahoo's price crash in 2000 big time, but he protected over $1 billion in cash by using a collar.

I recently had lunch with Mark and, among other things, reminisced about those times. King was so correct, but that is water under the bridge. The so-called Internet stock crash occurred in early April 2000. My paper net worth was no longer at the billion-dollar level, and by the end of 2000, the stock of my Internet.com was $6 a share vs. Close to $80 a share in the first quarter of 2000. I still had a significant paper net worth, and felt confident that I would see a robust stock price in coming years. In 2005, the price of my stock reached about $25 a share, and the same was my changing the thrust of operations to selling stock photos online. The billion dollar mark was not going to be attainable again.

I have not been bothered by this history. My only regrets concerning my net worth have more to do with taking the wrong fork in the road in meetings with Jon Oringer when he started Shutterstock, not going with my gut instinct to purchase iStockphoto in 2004-5, and not selling Jupiterimages to Corbis and Bill Gates in 2005. In each case, either underlings or my board of directors talked me out of executing on these options. The Jack Ma meeting in October 1999 in Hong Kong, and our breakfast about his business plan, can be looked at as a big mistake too. However, as I have mentioned, my Internet.com stock at the time was jumping in price daily, and I had little need to push Jack for an investment in Alibaba, having sold Mecklermedia a year earlier.

The lesson in all this is that hubris is always present when an entrepreneur is hitting on all cylinders. These are times when it is helpful to have a trusted and experienced financial advisor, one who will hopefully warn of the pitfalls around the corner. I had such an advisor, who tragically died a few years before 2000. At the time I made my poor decisions, I did not have that type of advisor. And today, as I do venture capital, I warn startup entrepreneurs that money is their most important asset, that they should not think the next multi-million-dollar raise will always be there for the asking.

DYSLEXIA

I am dyslexic, but did not know this until I was 55 years old. I always knew I had trouble with certain subjects, including multiple choice tests, college boards, and algebra. In fact, I never passed algebra in high school. As a youngster, I was almost forced to repeat the second grade because I could not read. Fortunately, I taught myself to read the baseball sports section of the daily New York newspapers, having become fascinated by baseball. In the sixth grade, I was admonished for writing a paper on King Henry VIII because I wrote the paper spelling Henry as "Herny." I remember the teacher reading my paper to the entire class and being continuously laughed at as he emphasized "Herny." Through it all, I had an incredible memory and memorized words and spellings, creating mental paths to overcome my problems. Nobody told me I had a problem because most schools in the 1950s didn't know much about learning disabilities. I just knew I was different, knew I could excel at history, and took satisfaction in what I could do best.

The other problem I had to overcome was not being able to organize thoughts. If I retold a story, I would jump out of sequence, but realizing this, I trained my mind to stay on course. In the end, I became a good public speaker. I was fortunate that I went to a strict boarding school where public speaking was emphasized and where the teachers helped me with my problems. But never was the word "dyslexia" mentioned. I was given low marks, but passed the subjects I could not master while getting top grades in any course where memorizing facts was a priority. I picked my subjects carefully in college and ultimately received a Ph.D. in American history from Columbia University.

The diagnosis of my dyslexia came from Sally Shaywitz, then the head of the Charles Schwab Center at Yale University for the study of dyslexia, when a freelance writer for *The New York Times* was doing a story about me. Coincidentally, this reporter was also working on another project about successful business dyslexics.

As he discussed examples of dyslexia with Dr. Shaywitz, my name came to mind, as I had told him my story about almost having to repeat the second grade because I could not read. It was an amazing day. On first hearing this pronouncement about my being dyslexic, I was, of course, a denier. But as he went on, I had an "aha moment" and realized he was correct. There followed a sense of calm and relief.

I later spoke to Professor Shaywitz and learned more about my condition. And then many things made sense to me that I had suppressed for 40 years or more. This explained the way I organize my work and my prodigious memory, as well as how I visualize new technologies and how I am able to spot trends in a visionary way. It also explained why I could not read certain types of charts—other than pie charts and bar graphs — and how I liked to have balance sheets described to me, rather than read them myself. And, finally, it explained how I conduct business meetings with my employees, where I keep everything brief and to the point, because I am able to listen and get salient points without having to spend much time on a presentation, whether in person or in print.

No doubt, dyslexia explained my leaning toward gut-reaction decisions, rather than mulling over decisions for hours or days. True, gut reactions have caused me angst by hindsight, but overall I have been correct way more than incorrect in these activities. I also think having had teachers and others think I was stupid in my younger days helped me overcome the many rejections I faced with my startups, not to mention the put downs I faced when significant media company types turned me down in my quest to raise funds for *Internet World* and other endeavors. Rejection can be hard to take, but I now realize that I faced rejection of a different type in my preadolescent years, and even in my teen years, because of my inability to handle certain school tasks. I would not want anyone to go through what I faced, even from my parents, who thought I was lazy, and many teachers in grade school and middle school who thought the same of me. On the other hand, these snubs turned out to be a special kind of education and training that made a perfect test bed for an inveterate entrepreneur.

FLYING CONCORDE

Hypersonic travel will come someday. But until it is reality, my having flown on Concorde, the supersonic airliner that operated during the last 20 years of the 20th century, feels like a science fiction memory.

The speed of sound is about 650 mph. Concorde was flown at close to 1200 mph, dramatically reducing flight time between Europe and New York. (For a short time, it also flew from Europe to Singapore.) Boarding Concorde was a special experience because the boarding lounges had special entrances so that passengers did not have to mingle in general boarding areas with conventional flights. Instead, one would exit the special lounge directly onto Concorde. Only eight Concordes were built, and British Airways and Air France were the only carriers with these incredibly beautiful airplanes.

I probably logged 12 flights over the years on Concorde, and every time the occasion was for an important reason. In the 1980s, the pricing for a flight was expensive for those times, but not exorbitant like business or first class transatlantic flights are today. The plane was not particularly comfortable, but then again the flight only took about three hours or less to get across the Atlantic. Most of the times I took Concorde, it was not full.

The years between 1980 and 2000 were a heavy travel period for me. I had an office in London that I visited at least once a month. I could leave New York's JFK Airport at about 10 a.m. and be in London for an early dinner, including the two-and-a-half hour flight and the five hour time change. Or I could leave London before 10 a.m. and be back in New York at the start of the business day.

It is incredible to think that travel such as this is now a relic from another era. Concorde ceased operations after the one and only crash of an Air France flight on takeoff from DeGaulle airport in July, 2000. I have probably flown 1000 times or more since my first business flight in 1971. I have flown first class and economy, and have been to Asia 50 times. Australia 20 times, and countless other times to European destinations. Nothing will ever top the experience of Concorde.

Periodically, I go to the Intrepid Museum on the Hudson River in New York City to marvel at the Concorde that sits next to the Intrepid. As one approaches, it is hard to believe that the majestic aircraft was a *passenger* plane. On approach, one might guess it was a fighter bomber that sat a crew of 10 at most. Even when one gets very close, it is hard to believe it carried 100 passengers and crew. I was fortunate that my business experiences gave me the opportunity to be part of aviation history and to have flown Concorde.

"FINISHED WITH OPRAH"

I lost my big chance to be on the *Oprah Winfrey Show* in 1985. In fact, I turned down the appearance, and might well be the only person in history to turn down being on *Oprah*. The reason? I had taken one of my ideas at the time and turned it into a paperback book called *The Complete Guide to Winning Lotteries by Mail*.

At the time, when the lottery craze in America had struck gold, I was mostly publishing reference books for research libraries. When I learned that the New York State Lotto game could be played by subscription through the mail, I wondered how many of the Lotto games in the U.S. and Canada allowed subscription play (at the time, there were Lottos in only about 20 states and provinces; it was only later that lottery variations emerged).

I realized I had a great idea for a book, reasoning there must have been millions of people who would play subscriptions beyond their respective state or province, if they had a convenient means to do so. Normally, I published reference books and guides for research libraries, but this was clearly a consumer book, so I used my knowledge of book packaging and found several large publishers that wanted to publish my book. Dell paperbacks won the rights, giving me a $25,000 advance against future royalties, which to me at the time was a bonanza! I contacted every lottery agency, and soon had the forms to republish in a slight paperback. There was little writing needed: just instructions, an introduction explaining the history of Lotto, and how to subscribe in each locale. All was great. Dell did a first printing of about 50,000 copies, and the book was launched. I was on radio for interviews almost every day for two weeks. The excitement was extreme. That's when one of Oprah's producers got in touch with me, inviting me to be a guest on a special segment that would feature me, the governor of Illinois, and a person who had just won the first huge Lotto in Illinois (and North America) of about $50 million. I was to get a first class airfare, a chauffeured limo from O'Hare, and a suite at a downtown Hyatt for my appearance. The date was two weeks hence.

I could not believe my good fortune. Then bad news struck. Some Congresspeople, who were antilottery fever, found an obscure lottery law from the 19th century that forbade interstate playing of lotteries in the U.S. (America had its first lottery craze after the Civil War, when this law was passed). New legislation passed Congress rapidly, and all of the sudden my great idea, and my book, were destroyed. I was crestfallen, and my editor at Dell took the news badly too, as he had committed quite a bit of money to the project. I mulled over the situation and, as badly as I wanted to be on *Oprah*, I had to cancel.

I called the *Oprah* producer, who was incredulous that I would cancel. She told me they would move forward with the segment with the governor and the lottery winner without me, adding that I should reconsider. "I could not possibly go on national television in good faith and push my book, as I would be encouraging people to break a federal law," I told her. The producer would not quit, and finished the conversation by telling me, "You are a fool and you are finished with ever being on Oprah." I felt bad about not being on *Oprah*, but worse about not making a small fortune on royalties (the book sales had jumped on release).

While this was not a startup effort, it is an example of how my mind worked, and still works. I'm constantly looking for new ideas, whether they be one-offs, startups, or new products. Unfortunately, this good idea and effort went to waste, but it does have pleasant memories. I have not met Oprah and probably never will. If I do have the pleasure, I am sure she will remember the lottery segment. I look at this story like the proverbial fisherman talking about "the one that got away."

FAMILY MATTERS

An entrepreneur is a driven person. In my case, even when things were not going well (and I had years of such conditions), the ideas kept coming. Going to sleep at night was never a problem because, instead of counting sheep, I was thinking of improving existing projects or scheming about new ones.

I have already mentioned that I believe an entrepreneur has an awareness that those not inclined to entrepreneurship lack. This means that even when you are with your wife, your children, or both, business thoughts are bound to intersect with family matters. In my case, however, because I am a great multitasker, I was able to get home for family dinners and not bring business to the table or show it when helping with chores or putting our young children to bed.

I think I have a unique ability to hide my feelings and concerns (although my wife of now 50 years is able to discern worry on my face). I had so many years of no financial success that I was able to cover up and fool my wife most of the time. Even when big success arrived in the early 1990s, I was always cognizant that things could go wrong. This is where it is good for the entrepreneur to have a healthy dose of paranoia (another trait that I possess and which I have previously mentioned). It is also helpful to be optimistic, to think that all one has to do when things are going bad is to adapt.

My children were born between 1972 and 1980. The 1980s then became the first time financial pressure became acute. In 1980, I was able to sell 50 percent of my business to Swedish media investors. However, this money seemed to evaporate overnight because I was living in New York City and facing four private school tuitions. Also, the '80s was more of the same for me in business; lots of critical success but little to no financial return. None of my media ideas could reach critical mass. My children never missed a beat, as they never saw my doubts. My wife knew my anguish, which was always worse when monthly household bills had to be paid.

My adult children today remember but one thing from the days when they were aware in the 1980s. They jokingly tell me that I am a hopeless optimist. They remember me talking about some projects or business trips and hear my wife asking about possible outcomes or results. As they remember it, my answers always focused on the positive — even if, deep down, I was not sure of success.

Mix optimism with paranoia, multitasking and adaptability to make things palatable in your home life while you fight to become a successful entrepreneur. Through the years, I have come across hundreds of wannabe entrepreneurs, only to realize after meeting these dreamers that many do not possess all of these qualities. In a way, I wonder if deep down an entrepreneur in constant startup mode is really fully honest with themselves, and even more so with their family. Looking back, I know I am morally honest, but must confess that in order to keep things going forward, I probably was not honest with my wife, and certainly not with my children. It was better to keep them in the dark during dire times, for their own good. It was hardest during the early 1990s, when I was constantly being turned down in my attempts to raise money for my Internet endeavors. This was the toughest time for my wife, as I projected optimism despite often being in shock and depressed by countless, negative outcomes and encounters. She had to wonder if I was crazy when I reported a negative result, and then watched me go out to try again and again. My children, who then ranged from 10 to 18 years of age, were protected from these disappointments. But my wife was a real trooper; she'd just listen and roll her eyes, but say little to dissuade me from going forward.

These days, one of my children, my son, works with me on venture capital projects, as well as my efforts to create another media company covering emerging technology in the additive manufacturing and quantum technology fields. I still have all the same traits that I had back then, and he too often bites his tongue when we have had a meeting or consider a proposed idea that I think has a great chance of success. I can get wildly optimistic quickly, and this can be off-putting to my son. Indeed, it might be better if we were not working together, since I am better able to hide disappointment on my own, when there isn't a family member watching me day by day or even minute by minute. On the other hand, I have always done well by having a wingman help me out, and my son is a whiz at handling the details that I cannot stomach. I thrive when there is someone I can trust so that I can think big picture and keep developing a project knowing that the smaller, but important, details will be covered.

MEDIA MOGULS/
BANKERS

FIRST DIBS ON ALIBABA

Beijing and the Internet in October 1999 was the equivalent of the 1849 gold rush in California. It was a time when most Chinese did not have landlines, and mobile phones were becoming the go-to method of communicating. No more than one million Chinese were Internet connected.

Out of the blue, I received an email from Micah Truman. Micah had been living in Beijing since 1994, after graduating from college. Micah and his business partner, Byron Constable (an Englishman), had a startup called Made For China and ran a monthly meetup in Beijing for those interested in the Internet. Both were 20-somethings, and were infatuated with the idea of making Internet riches in China. They were true pioneers. The duo decided to invite me to speak about Internet entrepreneurship, go over my experiences, and opine about where I thought Internet investing was headed. I was offered an air ticket and hotel accommodations to make the trek from New York City.

In those days, there was only one non-stop flight daily from the United States to China on Northwest Airlines out of Detroit. I remember eagerly looking forward to the trip and giving the talk, as this would also allow me to make my first visit to mainland China and to see the Great Wall and the Forbidden City. My wife accompanied me for three days in Beijing, then on to Hong Kong for a keynote at an Internet World show, which I had sold by this time, and then time at my Hong Kong office.

My schedule in Beijing was tight. Our flight was somewhat late, and the meetup speech was scheduled for 7 p.m. Micah and Byron met us at the Beijing airport. It was a hectic scene at the airport terminal, a very small cinder block building, probably built after World War II. We were hustled into a very small car and driven directly to the event hall, which was a free-standing building that appeared to be a party/restaurant hall. I was escorted to the stage and lectern, where I was amazed to find myself in front of about 500 excited Chinese and expat Internet entrepreneurs. There was palpable excitement in the hall. I could sense a thirst for information from the crowd, which was overwhelmingly composed of young Chinese men.

Looking back, I have no doubt that many of today's Chinese tech billionaires were sitting in that audience. I know for sure that Jack Ma was present, as we shall see. My talk then, as always, was completely extemporaneous, with a 3x5-inch card as my companion. I have never been able to do public speaking any other way, and this time was no different. I spoke for about 45-minutes, and Micah, who was fluent in Chinese, opened the floor for questions. With adrenaline pumping and the excitement of the moment, I could have gone on for hours, answering questions from eager attendees. In most cases, Micah had to translate for me, both the questions and my answers.

Later, after going to a Hutong for dinner in Beijing, we were driven to what was the first modern Western hotel in the heart of Beijing. The sparkling new St. Regis was the forerunner to an incredible building boom in Beijing and all over China. Within 30 minutes of settling into our lovely room at the St. Regis, I started getting phone calls from people in the lobby. It never occurred to me that when I offered, at the end of my talk at the meetup, to look at business plans that *hundreds* of people wanted to take me up on my offer. Over 100 entrepreneurs (Chinese and Western) were camped out in the lobby of the hotel. They started calling me in my room to meet in the lobby so I could advise them about their respective business plans. Soon, the hotel front desk or manager called to say they were going to turn off my phone in order to stop the crush of calls coming to my hotel room.

When my wife and I went to the lobby for breakfast the next morning, dozens more entrepreneurs crowded us, begging for me to check out business plans. I checked a few for 15 minutes, then had breakfast, and then went off to the Great Wall. This scene lasted for three days. I would come in from touring or descend into the lobby to find dozens of business plans thrust at me. It was a wild and memorable few days.

On my last night in Beijing, at dinner with Micah and Byron, I was asked to speak with David Oliver, who wanted a favor of me. David was a rugged fellow from New Zealand, an ex-professional rugby player. I subsequently called David, and the favor he requested was memorable: "I have a Chinese friend who I have been working with who has been camping out in the lobby of the St. Regis for three days and dearly wants you to check out his business plan," he said. Of course, I felt badly that this unnamed fellow had spent so much time trying to get my attention. I told David that I was leaving early the next morning for Hong Kong for three days, adding that if his friend could make it to Hong Kong, I would have plenty of time to chat, read the plan, and then discuss it. David checked with his friend and called back to say the two of them could meet for breakfast or lunch on one of my days in Hong Kong. And so it was agreed that two mornings hence we would meet for breakfast at the Mandarin Oriental. And this is how I met Jack Ma.

It was early morning as I entered the Mandarin's dining room. The Mandarin Oriental was one of the grand hotels of Hong Kong, sitting close to the harbor. I imagine that my guest had never been to such a majestic hotel at this point in his life. And since he considered me, in 1999, to be an important Internet entrepreneur, I am sure the setting impressed him.

I saw David, who was easy to spot being, as I remember it, well over 6 feet with blondish hair. Sitting next to him on the banquette was a rather small and almost odd-looking fellow, Jack Ma. After exchanging pleasantries, Jack told me in accented English that he had recently raised $60,000 from friends and family to launch his new business, Alibaba. Any educated person knew the name Alibaba, so I thought, as Jack handed me his business plan, "What could this be?"

The plan was in a plastic cover, and I gave it a quick read. My first reaction was "this will work," and so, cutting to the chase, I said to Jack, "This is Amazon for China." Jack agreed with a big smile and some word like "exactly." Jack went on to tell me how he had raised the funds and that he was hard at work on starting the company. He also told me that I was the first Internet Westerner to see the business plan, and that he was seeking my validation and opinion. I told him in no uncertain terms that the idea was a great one, and at that particular point in time, in China's pre-Internet-boom, he had a winner if he could execute. I then said, "I would like to invest $50,000 or more." Jack smiled and politely told me again that he had raised $60,000 recently, and that he had more than enough funding to last quite a while. So he declined my kind offer.

I remember sitting there thinking it was a great opportunity that I was losing out on. But on that particular morning, I had recently sold my first public company for $274 million cash; my second public company, Internet. com, had a market cap that morning of close to $700 million. So my net worth that morning approached well over $500 million. Also, if queried, I would have told anyone that morning that I was now well on the road to becoming a billionaire. What did it matter if Jack would not take my investment? Looking back, I look foolish, but that is with the aid of hindsight. My morning with Jack, however, is as memorable as being in Beijing in the Wild West Internet days. As for David Oliver, my understanding is that he was one of Alibaba's first 10 employees, and that he was granted significant stock options. I am told that when it came time to vest his pre-IPO options for the sum of a few thousand dollars, he declined, walking away from Alibaba with no money from his then-close association with Jack Ma.

Of all my memories of the early Internet days, the Jack Ma China trip is perhaps the most memorable. Much like having the opportunity to make a quick billion with Jon Oringer and Shutterstock, the decision taken at the time proved to be incorrect. Mostly, the fork in the road taken at the point was based on reasoning of facts and conditions made at the particular time in my history. The lesson is that when faced with investment decisions, whether personal or business, one should try to think outside the box and not just by the then-present numbers.

BIG BANKS

During my nearly 50-year career as an entrepreneur, I have come across some dumb and dishonest people. They come from all levels of the business community. But one would never expect that the private client division of a large New York bank was ground zero for some of the thickest and most dishonorable people I ever dealt with.

In late 1999, I was contacted by a career private client executive. The bank had as a client a wealthy New York attorney, who had become friendly with me and had invested in my first VC fund from Internet.com. The first fund of $5 million had a huge success with a company called Auction Rover. We then started Fund II, and raised $15 million, with the bulk of this funding coming from about 50 employees at investment bank Piper Jaffray.

The banker from Private Client thought he might be able to raise $150 million in short order from clients interested in the Internet boom. The proposed VC fund would be based on my conservative philosophy of not seeking Internet IPO candidates, but rather seeking start-ups that could be sold to large media companies for many times our investment. (Over time, my theory proved correct.)

A deal was struck. The bank put me on the road to meet clients across the U.S. and around the world, including stops in Hong Kong, Geneva, London and Paris. After just 30 days, we had commitments for $150 million. I was not astonished by the fundraising success. By this time in my journey, I had nothing but success with every idea and venture, starting with the launch of Internet World in 1993. And I had had success with Internet.com Fund I and II. Even though they were small funds, due to my outside-the-box philosophy of not seeking IPOs, I had been successful. Tackling a larger fund was exciting, and I started hiring personnel to help manage the enterprise.

But in late March 2000, about two weeks before the paperwork was finished on the fund, the 2000 Internet stock crash occurred. Like many financial "shocks" the warning signs were rampant but not heeded. Several Internet IPOs took place from 1995 to early 2000, and it was common for an IPO to rise several hundred percent on the first day of trading. A front page story in *Barron's* in the late March of 2000 demonstrated that the cash burn rate over 200 recent IPOs was not sustainable, and this sparked the crash in valuations. My company at the time, Internet.com, even though profitable and not burning cash, did not escape the carnage. The stock price plunged from near $70 a share to under $10 in short order.

The crash gave some clients cold feet, so our $150 million fund became $75 million by its April closing.

All was well for a few months. Our first investment was a fledgling website called HOW STUFF WORKS, which was followed by Tutor.com. The typical investment was $300,000 to $500,000, for 10 to 15 percent of the start-up's equity.

Several months and 10 fund investments later, I received a call from my contact to meet at his offices. This was not unusual; I regularly had congenial meetings with him and his colleagues at the bank.

The meeting was anything but congenial! Another employee appeared for the first time and abruptly told me the Internet was "a fraud" and that not only were values crashing on the stock market, but that start-ups were worthless. Those "worthless" equities, he added, included the positions we had taken in the Internet.com fund backed by the bank.

Then came the demands. The bank wanted out, wanted us to disband the fund posthaste and return uninvested funds immediately. The bankers accused me that "my game" was to get the 2 percent management fee, and that I had no regard for their clients.

I had no choice but to comply, as the bylaws for the fund gave the bank the ability to close the fund on demand. We had invested approximately $22 million of the $75 million fund. The bank wanted its money back immediately, and would not consider leaving even $5 million in the fund to help buttress some of the more promising portfolio companies.

The bank dumped its investments to a Dutch firm for a paltry $100,000. Years later, one of our start-up investments, HOW STUFF WORKS.COM, was sold to Discovery Networks for $250 million! And Tutor.com was sold for close to $50 million. Several other portfolio companies were sold for handsome returns. I doubt Doug or David had a clue about these later sales, as they were basically company men with no power, and had the backing of the head of the private client division, who threatened me with legal action if I did not readily comply. They essentially raped their clients and cost them huge returns.

ONE SMART INVESTMENT BANK

I had a four-year "affair," starting in 1995, with Allen & Company, the investment bank known mostly for its annual, week-long Sun Valley Conference every July and numerous media deals. Nancy Peretsman, a partner, got in touch with me soon after the public offering of Mecklermedia in February 1994. She knew little to nothing about the Internet back then, but was thirsting for more knowledge. She was one of the few if only investment bankers at the time who thought about the coming Internet boom and recognized I was ahead of the curve. Our first meeting was the start of an intense business relationship with Peretsman and her colleagues, with whom I met almost every two weeks for several years.

Many of these meetings were in the New York City Fifth Avenue office of Allen & Company. Typically, they would begin with an informal lunch of sandwiches, in a private dining room filled with Frederic Remington and Charles Russell paintings of the wild west worth millions of dollars. Peretsman would invite a variety of staffers and clients to meet me and have me answer questions about the Internet and where it was headed. It was, essentially, a continuous salon or seminar, with me as the guest lecturer, providing "Internet 101" basics and projecting my thoughts on stocks worth buying. I'll readily admit the meetings were exciting for me; besides, it was good to spread the word about Mecklermedia's stock, which was starting to ramp up from its February 1994 IPO price of $6.00 per share. In hindsight, I now realize Peretsman was grooming me and my company for a sale to some large media company — which would result in a nice commission for Nancy. I was soon being invited to the Allen & Company's "B" level annual conference, held at the Boulders Resort in Arizona, where I would give lectures on my Internet thoughts as well as Mecklermedia. Around the same time, I was told that I was destined to be included in Allen & Company's Sun Valley confab, the famous annual July gathering of mega media and investor types, such as Barry Diller, Bill Gates, Warren Buffett and dozens more.

The Peretsman saga continued for years, as she tried mightily to broker a deal to sell Mecklermedia or to have us buy other media properties. Nancy came close to getting Pat McGovern, founder of International Data Group, to purchase Mecklermedia a few times. Unfortunately, while Pat was a big talker about spending money, his practice was to offer a bundle of cash for a deal and then deliver a memorandum of understanding that offered little cash along with some type of asset swap or partnership. That didn't interest me or Nancy.

Peretsman did introduce me to Sir Clive Hollock, then CEO of UK-based United Business Media. In the summer of 1998, she brokered a deal in which UBM would purchase Mecklermedia for approximately $290 million in cash. Hollock dragged his feet for weeks. Then the financial crisis known as "Russian default" hit and financial markets worldwide tumbled.

Hollock used this event as an excuse to drop the deal. Based on my conversations with Hollock, I think the real reason for backing out was his lack of "true belief" in the value and future of internet media. The tip-off was his desire to have me keep the Web assets of Mecklermedia (assets I later took public, and which ultimately attained over a billion dollar market cap).

In the end, Hollock was less than honorable. As for Nancy, she threw a fit when the deal collapsed and told me she "would never do business with Hollock again." But 12 months later, she brokered the deal in which CMP Media was sold to UBM and Hollock for about $1 billion. My feeling is that Hollock panicked after losing the Mecklermedia deal and then went out and grossly overpaid for CMP, which was worth about $500 million at most at the time. So, in the end, Peretsman got back at Hollock by selling him a "lemon" for dropping the Mecklermedia deal while getting a big commission for herself. And Hollock ended up with assets that had peaked in value years earlier.

Within days of UBM dropping the Mecklermedia deal, I was approached by Lou Freedman of the investment bank Donaldson, Lufkin & Jenrette (DLJ). Freedman said his client Penton Media would take over where

UBM had dropped off. Ten days later, the deal was done for $274 million in cash! However, Penton was also fearful of websites, so part of the deal was for me to obtain an 80.1 percent interest in the Mecklermedia website assets for $18 million. (Another chapter will delve into the economics of this deal and focus on how traditional media companies couldn't fathom the future of websites.)

In the end, I realized that Nancy Peretsman and Clive Hollock were less than honorable with me. Unfortunately, I was always too trusting and believed everything Peretsman told me. And, by the way, I never got the golden ticket to the Allen & Co. Sun Valley Conference.

GOING PUBLIC, 1994

After Jim Mulholland Sr. Invested $1.25 million in my company in August 1993, I thought I was "on my way" financially. But by September, I realized I was burning cash rapidly and that the Mulholland money was not going to be enough to market and grow our new Internet World magazine. So, in late September, I approached Mulholland about buying more stock at a higher valuation. Jim was a nice fellow, but a tough negotiator; he wanted control for the additional investment. Worried about losing control, I was not sure about next steps. And while I admired and was thankful for Jim's investment, I was saddled with his son, Jim III, who while very smart was incapable of doing the simplest task.

My retired father in Sarasota, Florida, who had had a brilliant mind, suggested that I chat with a friend of his who worked with a small investment bank in Denver that raised funds for small companies through public offerings. The suggestion seemed insane. It sounded like a so-called penny stock offering, and so I scoffed at the idea. However, I was again desperate for funds, and so I had phone call with my father's friend, Victor Kashner. Victor, who like my father was based in Sarasota, had a business relationship with Cohig, the investment bank in Denver.

Next I was introduced to Stephen Bathgate, CEO of Cohig. Bathgate mentioned that he and two Cohig colleagues would be in Boston in early October and that we should meet to discuss taking Meckler Publishing public. Off I went to the Boston meeting. I spent 30 minutes chatting up where the Internet was going and how Meckler Publishing could be in the middle of the Internet revolution through its trade shows and magazine.

One has to remember that in the fall of 1993, suggesting there was going to be an Internet revolution was preposterous. After all, several significant media kings— Hippeau, Leeds, Cron, and others—had passed on my ideas. I had the feeling the Cohig boys were in the same doubter camp.

Lo and behold, after I finished my spiel, Bathgate said something like: "That is the most interesting concept I have heard in a long time. We can have you public in 90 days."

I was in shock!

I left Boston thinking that while Bathgate was very positive, Cohig was still an unknown. And I remained concerned about becoming a penny stock. Nonetheless, Bathgate threw out the idea I could get my hands on $5 million, so I had to take the idea seriously.

Back home, I turned to a friend who was the lead intellectual property lawyer at the prestigious New York law firm Weil Gotschal. My friend was skeptical, but set me up with one of the firm's SEC lawyers, an attorney named Steve. I sat down with Cooper and could immediately tell he did not want to spend too much time with me talking about a penny stock offering out of Denver. At one point, Steve stood up and started wiping his shoes on the carpet, as one would do after stepping in dog-crap. "This is what people will think of you and your company if you go public with a Denver firm like Cohig," he said. This hit home with me, of course, because I had some of the same concerns. After a day of thought, I decided to proceed. Where else was I going to get my hands on $5 million to carry on with my dream of making Internet World a huge financial success?

Thus I embarked on the road to an IPO. Only one as naïve as me could consider taking this route. The pitfalls were immense. But if you are a dreamer, a plugger, and a diehard entrepreneur, you take risks. The Mulhollands were not supportive, but because I'd wisely retained voting control of my company, I decided the public route was the way to go.

Another chapter will delve into my IPO experiences, which included getting knifed in the back by the attorney assigned to me by Weil Gotschal and an SEC examiner who was incredulous about the future of the Internet. The bottom line is that I saw a path to raise several million dollars after having been turned down by countless individuals and organizations who doubted my dreams. The guys at Cohig were heroes. Sure they wanted to make money, but they were the first commercial organization to buy my pitch about the coming

Internet Revolution. Without them, and their faith, Mecklermedia would not have been a success.

$30 MILLION—TAKE IT OR LEAVE IT

The December 1994 Internet World was a landmark success. The venue was a low-ceilinged exhibit hall at the Washington Hilton in Washington, D.C. Attendance was 5,000.

Exhibit space was sold out, thanks to IBM taking 10 booths (or 25 percent of the exhibit hall) to introduce to the world what IBM and its new president, Lou Gerstner, were betting would be "the next big thing," the Internet, and to announce that IBM was going into the Internet server business.

It was also the show at which Netscape went big, giving away thousands of disks that could get a new user connected to the Internet. And it was the show where Jerry Yang and David Filo, the founders of Yahoo, agreed to place Yahoo on my new website, MecklerWeb. (More on this in a later chapter.)

Things were so wild at the show that we ran a seminar titled "How to Connect to the Internet" about six times in three days, and still had hundreds of attendees clamoring for admission.

About a week after the completion of the show, I got a call from Ziff Davis' CEO Eric Hippeau. Only a year earlier, Hippeau had felt that the Internet was "nothing more than a modem." But now he wanted to buy my magazine, Internet World.

Eric got right to the point. "I am offering you $30 million cash for the magazine, and if you do not accept I will start a Ziff Davis competitor and crush you!"

Since the last time I'd met with Eric in 1993, my company had gone public, Internet World was growing rapidly, adding over 150,000 paid subscribers in one year, and the Internet World trade show was well into the black, doubling in sold exhibit space and tripling in paid attendance every six months. And my stock was worth about $10 million. Even so, I had very little personal cash.

"I doubt you can overtake my magazine," I told Eric, "and even if I would sell, I cannot because the magazine and the show are attached."

"Look," I continued, "I have what Bill Ziff had in the beginning of the PC revolution, the largest magazine, but I *also* have what Sheldon Adelson had with Comdex, the largest computer trade show. I cannot sell only one. It would have to be the show *and* the magazine. Make it $50 million and I will take it to my board."

At this point, an aid jumped in on the conversation and told his boss, "Hold it, Eric, my understanding is that the show in D.C. was just so-so, and I am not sold on the future of the Internet."

"Were you in Washington?" I responded. "No," the aid said. "Your intelligence on the show is off by 180 degrees," I said.

With that, Eric said that his new owners (Forstman Little & Company, a private equity firm) did not want to be in the trade show business, but that he would check with them. He also said his CFO, Tom Thompson, who was present at the meeting, to do four weeks of due diligence, after which he would get back to me to see if we could make a deal.

We fed Thompson and his team answers to all their questions.

Four weeks later, Thompson called me. "After due diligence, we here at Ziff just do not think that the Internet is going to be that big," he said.

Later, Ziff launched a few different Internet publications to make good on Eric's threat. They all failed.

MUTUAL FUND MANAGERS

An entrepreneur has to be a salesman. This helps in numerous ways, from raising funds, to selling products, to advertising. Or, if you're a public company, to selling your stock to mutual funds and other investors.

My career has encompassed two IPOs and three secondaries, as well as launching a mutual fund. IPOs and secondaries require roadshows in which the CEO and CFO travel for about two weeks with Wall Street bankers, meeting the potential buyers of the offered stock. Most of these buyers, at least during my roadshows, were mutual fund managers. And after the IPO, it is not uncommon to do mini roadshows or selected presentations.

I estimate I have made more than 600 hundred of these presentations. An IPO roadshow might encompass 75 presentations over an average of 10 to 12 days. In some cases, the roadshow took me to England and Europe, as well as across the USA. My first experience was the IPO for Mecklermedia in early 1994, which was handled by Cohig, a small firm based in Denver. Looking back, it was the most fun and most interesting experience I had with all of my roadshows. First, it was a new experience and I did not know what to expect. Second, the Cohig team was lots of fun and incredibly enthusiastic. Finally, I was teaching people about the beginnings of the commercial Internet. In 12 days on the road, I do not think I came across one person who had ever heard of the Internet. (Remember, this was early 1994.) Very few questions were asked as I made these presentations across the United States. People were, I presume, dumbfounded. I presume many listeners were non-believers but, fortunately, on the day of the IPO someone from GE Capital purchased several hundred thousand shares.

A roadshow presentation is essentially the same in every case. Over 12 days, you might meet with 75 fund managers or investors. As you might expect, after a while, you get into rhythm and know within a minute if you are connecting or not with your listener. It can be a grind to do this day after day, so having fun bankers who travel with you for support is a must and very helpful for getting through the days.

When I look back over those 600 presentations, one fund manager stands out more than any other: Winthrop Knowlton. Win Knowlton's family was media-centric, as several Knowltons were associated with the old-line publishing house of Harper & Row.

Win understood exactly what we were attempting to do and what we were trying to become. His questions were always perceptive. I imagine his firm made many millions on Mecklermedia, and later on my Internet.com. My only regret about meeting with Win was that he told me to buy shares in Audible, the seller and producer of audio entertainment, information, and programming, when it was selling at about 50 cents a share. Win was a big holder and believer. But I did not get it for some reason, and so lost out on making many millions by not becoming an Audible investor. (Today, Audible is part of Amazon, which purchased it in March 2008 for around $300 million.)

Another interesting experience was with Royce Funds, founded by Chuck Royce and his number two, Whitney George. These guys understood our story for both Mecklermedia and Internet.com and made millions. It was interesting with Royce, who is still around. He used to call me several times a year to bend my ear about startups he wanted to invest in or other public plays in the Internet space. We certainly were not friends, but when I saw him recently at a conference and introduced myself, he had no time to say hello.

This was a lesson about fund managers, whose attitude is usually, "What have you done for me lately?" It is easy to get taken in by the exuberance these managers show you if they are making money with you, but then how quickly they forget you if things go south. I foolishly used to think these guys liked me, but of course this was naïve.

Another interesting memory is Joe McNey, who ran Essex Funds in Boston. I must have had 10 one-on-ones with him and his associates in the 1990s. He would pump me for my stock picks in the go-go Internet days.

When I last saw him around 2011 or so I doubt he remembered how intense his interest was in me when he could make money. Again, it was very naïve of me.

CLASS ACTION LAWSUIT GARBAGE

As CEO of public companies from 1994 through 2015, I prided myself on overseeing honest business operations. As a public company in the era of Sarbanes-Oxley, a CEO must be very conscious of the legal consequences of not complying with SEC regulations. Every quarter, a CEO is required to sign a legal document stating that he or she has complied with the accounting and legal requirements set down by the SEC and other government agencies. Nevertheless, on several occasions, my companies faced legal actions known as class action lawsuits.

Class action lawsuits are created by law firms who claim to represent every stockholder, but in reality are generally legal fictions created by specialized law firms, who start these actions using America's legal system to, in a sense, blackmail a public company. Once sued, these companies typically settle to avoid facing months or years of costly litigation. No doubt some of these claims have a semblance of truth, but generally the law firm finds a stockholder with a minimal number of shares — one who never dreamt of starting a legal action — and then uses this person as the face of the suit. Law firms bringing these actions are aware that every public company has what is known as "directors and officers insurance," and counts on the policy having been written in such a way to settle legal actions rather than face years of paying claims under the terms of the insurance policy, which protects the company's directors and officers rather than the company itself. Once a settlement is reached, usually for millions of dollars, the law firm ends up with the lion's share of the financial settlement. Meanwhile, the stockholders, the "class" in the class action, get a very small percentage of the payout.

One such claim against one of my companies came from then the then well-known firm of Milberg Weiss, which was known for existing only to bring class action lawsuits. A reading of the claim against Mecklermedia was one part fact and 99 parts fiction. Milberg Weiss found a stockholder from Brooklyn, New York, who had 100 shares of our public company. The claim was that I and several so-called insiders benefited from the creation of Internet.com and its public offering, and that I and others cut out other Mecklermedia stockholders. After the case dragged on for a few years, and after legal bills reached $1 million, the insurance company for our directors and officers policy settled by paying Milberg Weiss about $7 million. Interestingly, not long after this settlement, several principles of Milberg Weiss were sent to jail for fraud. It turned out they were essentially paying off small stockholders (like the one who sued Mecklermedia) to front as an "injured" stockholder. In reality, without paying off such a person, there would not have been a legal action. Another case against my company Jupitermedia came from a firm in Philadelphia. In 2007, they claimed that I, several officers, and the board had backdated stock option plans so that we could benefit from stock price swings and get better payouts. There was a flurry of such actions by this firm and others, and again it was a great means for them to make a bundle of money while stockholders received fractions of what the law firm pocketed. In this case, unfortunately, the filing occurred just as Getty Images was preparing to close on purchasing the image business of Jupitermedia (Jupiterimages) for $375 million in cash. The filing occurred as we were publishing and filing our quarterly financials. When Getty saw the legal filing, they canceled the deal, arguing that they had based their offer on Jupitermedia having certified quarterly numbers. They undoubtedly also feared that the legal action might last for many months or years. Outside legal and accounting firms were brought in and exonerated our officers and directors of breaking regulations on backdating. Nonetheless, it was too late, and the Getty deal disappeared. The hucksters in Philadelphia got a $750,000 insurance payoff settlement, which they would have lost if their suit had gone to trial. But my stockholders got screwed, as the class action payoff was miniscule compared to what the payout would have been from the Getty Images deal. I probably lost about $100 million due to this class action legal fiction.

My feeling then and now is that our American legal system encourages legal blackmail because the U.S. does not follow the United Kingdom's system, where "loser pays" is the norm. With loser pays, the party bringing a lawsuit or class action as plaintiff has to pay the defendant's legal costs, if the defendant is found not guilty. What a pity loser pays is not part of the American legal system. Not having this in place means a fortune is wasted on insurance premiums by every business, every professional and more. This is one of several items that should have been passed by Congress long ago, but then Congress is full of attorneys, and loser pays would clearly hurt the legal profession's billings. So we all suffer.

IPO ROADSHOW STORIES

From 1993 to 2014, I oversaw two IPOs, three secondaries, and the public launch of a mutual fund . Several Wall Street banks participated in these offerings.

Denver-based Cohig was the first bank I used for Mecklermedia's 1994 IPO; Pacific Growth handled Mecklermedia's secondary in 1995. Piper Jaffray was the lead banker for the Internet.com IPO in June 1999, and Hambrecht & Quist, which had been acquired a few months earlier by Chase Manhattan, ran the secondary for Internet.com in January 2000, followed by Piper Jaffray again for a secondary under the Jupitermedia brand in May 2004. My mutual fund, 3DPrinting Technology Fund, was launched in 2014, piloted by the law firm Dechert.

An IPO or secondary takes months to prepare for and complete. Specialized attorneys and accountants are needed, and there is endless inter-action with the Securities and Exchange Commission attorneys. After getting the documentation in order, a "road show" takes place in which the CEO and CFO, with accompanying Wall Street bankers, visit perhaps 10 cities, where they make the same presentation to investors (usually mutual fund managers). Over a two-week period there are about eight presentations a day. In some cases, a road show would take me to Switzerland or to England. The appetite for Internet IPOs in the late 1990s into the spring of 2000 was insa-tiable, so it was common for road shows to spend time, particularly in Geneva, Switzerland and London, England. There was not much difference from a presentation abroad versus one anywhere in the United States. Of course, the time changes made for much exhaustion.

The road show process is exhausting, and there were times during a grueling day of eight presentations when I felt like saying, "I cannot possibly do the same presentation yet again." Every once in a while, a fund manager would stand out for asking bright questions or exhibiting a sense of humor. But it was not unusual to find a skeptic, and for the presentation to turn ugly. This happened once on a California swing. A noted bank representative got into a debate with me when I claimed that another Internet company, EarthWeb, which was competitive with Internet.com, used barter revenues extensively, whereas my company did not. For this reason, I felt we were the superior operation. Similarly, I used to compare Internet.com with a company called VerticalNet. VerticalNet had a market capitalization many times the size of Internet.com, but I felt that VerticalNet's business model was flawed to the point of absurdity, whereas Internet.com had a totally legitimate operation that could be sustained.

During my secondary road show for Internet.com, in late January 2000, I remember that VerticalNet announced that it was doing a special deal with Microsoft. Its stock jumped close to $200 that day! When asked about this by a fund manager at a roadshow presentation, I said, "VerticalNet is close to being fraudulent." In my view, their model, which portrayed the company creating hundreds of storefronts for different industries, was a deception. VerticalNet had a water vertical, a poultry vertical and many other disjointed verticals. Investors and day traders bought into the concept, feeling that every one of these verticals would be financially successful, and VerticalNet's market cap jumped to about $10 billion or so. My retort was that VerticalNet could not be successful because, other than its software, there could be no integration; that one vertical did not sell another. And because they were so disjointed, it would end up being a huge cash flow drain. When the Internet crash came in April 2000, VerticalNet was decimated as it was "burning" money rapidly.

My main assertion about VerticalNet came from the lesson I learned from 1972 to 1994: all for one and one for all, and that focus was needed to be successful as a startup or in any young business. I had a favorite line about VerticalNet: The only connection between the water vertical and the poultry vertical is that chickens drink water." On the other hand, if a fund manager held VerticalNet in his portfolio, I obviously was not going to be viewed positively if I trashed this stock, so I had to feel my way gingerly in some of these meetings, particularly if a portfolio manager asked my opinion about another Internet stock.

I had more interactions with the Minneapolis based firm of Piper Jaffray than any other Wall Street bank. I did three road shows with the firm, and in almost all cases, the lead banker was Chad Abraham. Chad was a perfect banker. Blonde, good looking and extremely personable. He was a great "customer man." In the end, when things went a bit south during the financial crisis, Chad and Piper dropped me quickly — to the point that neither phone calls or emails were answered. The high point with Piper was meeting a genius Internet stock analyst named Safa Ratschy. Safa was an Egyptian immigrant who was a junior analyst when I first got connected to Piper in 1999. The original analyst for our Internet.com offer was another fellow named Haine Nada. Nada soon left, and I was told Safa was taking on the role of analyst for Internet.com. My reaction was negative, as I thought this was a "bait and switch." In time, I came to realize that Safa was genius material and that he was a true student of Internet stocks, who realized the difference between hype and a solid business model. In later years, Safa was, I believe, the first analyst to understand the Google model, seeing it in a Google forerunner called Overture. Overture grew out of the concepts developed by Bill Gross' IdeaLab. Gross was ridiculed, but he proved to be the father of paid search (for which he is not recognized today).

Overture was a dollar stock in early 2002 or so when Safa started raving about it and the future of paid search. Ultimately, this stock jumped in value many times before Yahoo bought Overture. In fact, I dare say that Yahoo was "saved" by purchasing Overture, which made the reputation (undeserved) of Terry Semel, who became head of Yahoo at about this time, after a career in Hollywood. Overture is what turned around Yahoo, not Terry Semel. In fact, Terry supposedly had the opportunity to buy Google about this time. As the story goes, the Google deal was made, and then he backed out. I whiffed on some big decisions, but missing Google is the whopper of all time!

My Piper years had some great memories. I had become a bit of a rock star at Piper headquarters, and by the time I started venture capital funds as part of Internet.com; over 50 Piper employees placed anywhere from $15,000 to $25,000 into our Fund II in 1999. Fund II was brought down by the debacle caused by JPMorgan Private Client group in late 2000, when this group demanded I close down Fund III (a story that's related elsewhere in this book). However, Fund II's largest Limited Partner (LP) was a New York City attorney, who had placed $2 million into Fund II and an equal amount into Fund III. He was very close to JPMorgan management, and when they decided to close down Fund III, this attorney jumped on the bandwagon that the Internet was "a fraud" and demanded to withdraw funding from Fund II as well. This action caused me to have to shut down both Fund II and Fund III. The Piper investors all lost their investments, and also missed out on the ultimate big sale of infotainment website HowStuffWorks, a Fund II and Fund III investment, when it sold for $250 million a few years later.

The best time I ever had on a road show was with the small firm Pacific Growth, then based in San Francisco. I have no idea where the young bankers who worked this offering are these days, but Gary Cohn and Ben Houston were great traveling companions and really "got" the investment story of Mecklermedia in the summer of 1995.

The lesson in most of this is that, unfortunately, making money makes for strange bedfellows. There is a type of bonding, much like being on a baseball team or being in basic training, that happens on a road show. The connection is strong for a short period of time, and then just as quickly is gone. The fledgling entrepreneur should remember the lesson of staying a bit paranoid in all interactions, no matter how sincere the characters might be.

CHARACTERS

DEALING WITH A GIANT

Pat McGovern became a billionaire by building a tech media empire. However, in 1994, he and one of his chief aides, Pat Keneally, very much wanted CD-ROM World, a magazine I had created in 1992 that was the leading newsstand and subscription magazine covering the use of CD-ROM.

By the end of 1993, my Meckermedia had three tech magazines: Internet World, Virtual Reality World and CD-ROM World. McGovern and his IDG resented my use of "World" in my titles, claiming on more than one occasion that we had no right to the term. It was a ridiculous claim (IDG ultimately sued Mecklermedia), as there were dozens of magazines in the U.S. that used "World" in their respective titles. Essentially, McGovern and IDG were arguing that if a publisher had a good idea in the tech space, IDG had rights to it. This was nonsense. (Even today, years after Pat's death in 2014, IDG continues to pursue my present company because we own the URL iWORLD (a domain that Steve Jobs tried to buy from us, but that's another vignette).

Back to the story. One day, Pat Keneally got in touch with me about Mecklermedia selling CD-ROM World to IDG. It was 1995, and my gut instinct was that CD-ROM was dead and the Internet was where the money was to be made. I played coy and said, "Sure, I'll sell CD-ROM World." And the IDG team took the bait! I suppose the two Pats figured a little library publisher could never compete with them as a trade magazine publisher. Apparently, neither of them had a clue about the future of the Internet. In this, they were similar to the Ziff Davis and CMP teams.

Over the protests of my largest stockholder, the Mulholland family, I made the decision to sell CD-ROM World. The money was not huge; our magazine lost money. However, in addition to giving me several hundred thousands of dollars, the two Pats gave me free access to the IDG direct mail database. I got the rights to use 1 million names, as well as ad placements in several IDG magazines, which would help me market Internet World.

The cute part of the deal was twofold: At a closing dinner in New York City, Pat Keneally told me both he and Pat McGovern were pleased with the deal, adding that they figured it would be less than a year before I would turn to them to sell my Internet World magazine. There was no way my model would be successful, Keneally predicted, because "I did not have the infrastructure to be a successful magazine publisher." The second cute part: both of the Mulhollands sent me a registered letter, telling me that selling CD-ROM World was a huge mistake and that, as the second largest stockholder, they demanded I sell all of Mecklermedia to IDG.

The Mulholland threat was a pain, and I disregarded their warning as a nuisance. I was convinced that Internet World was the path to success and wealth. I hated to go against the desires of Jim senior, but I knew I was on the right path, as CD-ROM was already failing as an important technology.

INTERNET GURU

I doubt there were more than 20 people in the world who could intelligently describe the concept of a website in December 1993. One of those 20 was a fellow named Chris Locke. Chris had been hired by CMP to edit a newsletter about using the Internet, but after a falling out with management (a common occurrence for Chris) he was terminated. I saw this as a great opportunity for Mecklermedia's efforts to bring experts together to validate our fledgling magazine, Internet World, and a trade show of the same name as best in the world.

Locke agreed to come onboard. I realized immediately that he was incredibly smart, but also a strongly opinionated person. We had been preparing our documents to go public (fall 1993) and indicated that we were going to launch what was known as an electronic bulletin board devoted to the topic of the Internet. I showed this to Chris and he immediately said, "Why not create a website to do the same thing?" I had no idea what a "website" was, and so Chris elaborated, selling me on the idea in a few minutes. Thus was born MecklerWeb (perhaps one of the first websites in the world). It was Chris' idea that MecklerWeb would be a catch-all for any industry that would benefit by having a website. In those days (December 1993), the idea of having a website meant spending at least $50,000 for a server. But Chris' view was that most organizations would not spring for an expensive server and, instead, would throw in with MecklerWeb, which would become a universal hub housing an unlimited number of organizations' Web presences. He further speculated that we could attract large companies as anchors for different industries. For example, there would be an advertising section and one of the larger agencies would pay Mecklermedia to become the lead of the vertical called "advertising." In fact, he immediately interested advertising agency Ogilvy & Mather to fill this role. Interestingly, the lead Internet person at Ogilvy was Martin Nissenholtz, who later built the Web assets of *The New York Times*.

The concept was brilliant for December 1993 and made for good reading. Indeed, Fortune magazine published an article about MecklerWeb that featured Chris. This was great press for our initial public offering, which occurred in early February 1994.

I soon realized that I had a "tiger by the tail" because the costs of trying to build out the Chris Locke model were going to impede my plans on growing Internet World magazine. Chris was undaunted in his quest to make MecklerWeb the leading website on the newborn World Wide Web. We began to clash. I saw MecklerWeb as a path to bankruptcy; Chris saw it as being worth millions, if not billions, of dollars. By the time we ran spring Internet World in San Jose, California, in April 1994, I realized Chris had to go or Mecklermedia would blow up because of the costs of running MecklerWeb.

When I let Chris go, the hard-core Internet professionals lambasted me and I was panned by Forbes magazine and professional publications who sided with him. But I saw MecklerWeb as a vertical magazine that would go hand in glove with our magazine and trade show, and which would cover only the business of the Internet. In hindsight, Chris' vision was brilliant, but not one we could develop. It was the forerunner to Amazon and many other horizontal megasites that exist today.

Chris went on to be hired by several large technology companies, including IBM. Not surprisingly, Chris never lasted more than a few months at any of these stops. He was not a company guy, but rather a brilliant original thinker, and so he could not tolerate a corporate environment. He was one of the authors behind the tech classic "The Cluetrain Manifesto," which examined the impact of the Internet on marketing. But he is now another of the forgotten early pioneers of the commercial Internet.

KATHERINE GRAHAM

One of my early supporters, who ultimately became a Mecklermedia board member, was Michael Davies. Michael had been, at one time, publisher of The Hartford Courant and The Baltimore Sun, and was well known in newspaper circles, and when I first met him he was an investment banker at Legg Mason in Baltimore.

As Mecklermedia became a power in the Internet space with its magazines and Internet World trade shows, we started to get unsolicited inquiries to see if the company would entertain a buyout. Inquiries came from a variety of trade show and media companies, and were handled by Allen & Company, our unofficial banker.

One day in late 1996, Michael suggested that his business friend Donald Graham of The Washington Post might be a perfect buyer. Sure enough, Graham was interested and invited Mike and me to The Washington Post offices for a discussion.

Graham was incredibly gracious at the first of several meetings. Things progressed rapidly and I was invited back to have lunch with Don and his mother Kathryn, which I took to mean a deal was imminent and that, if I passed muster with Don's mother, a deal was a certainty.

The lunch took place in the corporate dining room and seemed to go very well. But then, for whatever reason, discussions went sideways and the deal went south.

Talks were resurrected a few months later, but to no avail. I have always presumed that either Warren Buffet, a large stockholder in The Washington Post and not a technology champion, shot it down, or a failed CD-ROM deal had soured several Post executives and scared them about getting into another technology transaction. Regardless, things ended cordially and I had the great experience of meeting Donald and Kathryn.

VINTON CERF
AND THE
INTERNET SOCIETY

Vint Cerf is one of the "fathers" of the Internet. He is associated with Google these days. Cerf created many of the protocols that we all use for basic email and more.

In my early Internet days (1990-1992), as I sought subscribers for my Internet World newsletter and event, I was constantly trolling research magazines to find individuals or organizations that might want to support my endeavors. In one of these research magazines, I came across a story about Vinton Cerf and his new Internet Society, which he had founded to educate academics and others about email and how the Internet could be used (this was pre-World Wide Web, the hypertexted pages that can be accessed using a Web browser).

I wrote to Cerf and joined his Internet Society. In fact, I still have my membership card from 1992. After joining, I wrote to him again to ask if the society would endorse my Internet World newsletter and new event, and if I could send information about these properties to his membership. He responded testily, objecting to my wanting to commercialize the field. Needless to say, he did not cooperate in any fashion.

A few years later, I was invited to be a speaker at The Wharton School of the University of Pennsylvania, along with several Internet luminaries of the time. And there was Vint Cerf. And I must say that when he saw my name badge, he immediately came over to me and offered a very genuine apology for not seeing that I was on the right path in 1992. He said he had been somewhat blinded by what he considered to be "doing good."

Later that year, Vint was the keynote speaker at one of the early Internet World trade shows in Sydney, Australia, at Darling Harbour. One night, I happened to be at another table at a restaurant not far from where Vinton was seated. He sent over a great Australian Red!

ROBERT MAXWELL

My first publication was Microform Review, created in 1971. It was a quarterly journal that reviewed research materials published on microfiche and microfilm for the 3,000 academic and special libraries worldwide. It was critically and financially successful immediately.

The world of academic and scholarly publishing is lucrative, provided one can find a service or some vertical information that these libraries "need to have."

By 1980, Microform Review attracted the attention of Englishman Robert Maxwell, who owned hundreds of academic research journals and who went on to own several British and American newspapers. Maxwell was imposing in stature and ability. He could speak eight languages, won the Victoria Cross in World War II, and became a member of Parliament. Czech born, he escaped from the Nazis as a teenager and made his way to London, England. He died mysteriously at sea in the 1990s.

But back in 1980, if Robert Maxwell called you on the phone, you were impressed. He called me one weekend to say he wanted to purchase my small company and its various academic publications. He suggested we meet the following Friday at 10 a.m., in his suite at a hotel across from the United Nations. I appeared at the appointed hour and found several of his lieutenants. I was surprised to see this assemblage because Maxwell had clearly told me we would have a one-on-one negotiation. After exchanging pleasantries, his attorney and the others start to negotiate.

Maxwell then dropped in an hour later to find out how things were going. He was well over 6 feet tall, stocky, with slicked back black hair and huge eyebrows. He spoke in an elegant English accent. I was rattled by his presence and could hardly speak as my reaction on seeing him was I was meeting with the devil.

He was pleased that terms were almost agreed, and then announced that he had to have lunch with the then-Secretary General of the U.N. Kurt Waldheim. And he was gone.

Later that day the negotiations, for a variety of reasons, broke down over demands by the other side to be able to claw back part of the acquisition price if certain parameters were not achieved. At about this time, Maxwell reappeared with his daughter Ghislaine, obviously having been tipped off that there might be no deal. He threw open the door to the suite and flung his raincoat against the wall. Screaming at everyone to leave the room, he said, "Alan and I are going to make a deal." He gave me 10 minutes to agree.

There was no deal. It took great willpower on my part to be face-to-face with this rock star publishing magnate, but I held my ground. A week later, I got another weekend call from "Captain Bob," as he was known, from his estate in Oxford, England. But again, no deal was struck.

RAFAT ALI

Everyone in the Internet or digital media business knows Rafat Ali, even if one has not had the pleasure of meeting him. Born and raised in India, he brought his fledgling journalism skills to New York City and was hired by Jason Calacanis in the late 1990s to work on Silicon Alley Reporter. Back in those days, I was somewhat of a rock star in the media world because of the Internet World properties and the successful IPOs of Mecklermedia and Internet.com.

It seemed I was on the phone or emailing with Rafat or Jason every few weeks for a few years.

Rafat went on to create the "Bible" of Internet media deals with his PaidContent.org, which he ultimately sold to the British newspaper group Guardian Media Group.

PaidContent was an everyday must-read. And it was a must to feed advance information to Rafat—if one wanted the word out to the industry. He was a great interviewer, and was so smooth that it was easy to give him too much information.

Rafat today has a successful start-up called Skift.com that covers the travel, restaurant and industries in a unique fashion. (I was one of several angel investors when he launched a few years ago.)

To be a successful entrepreneur, it is good to have positive press relations and to professionally befriend the right people. Rafat, much like Jason, was a valuable sounding board in building some of my endeavors. And the Skift investment might have been one of my best.

SHELDON ADELSON
AND TAKING ON COMDEX

Sheldon Adelson is a multi-billionaire who made his first billion with a computer trade show he founded in the late 1980s called Comdex. He sold the show for close to $1 billion in cash to another billionaire, Masayoshi Son of Softbank, in 1994. Sheldon also owned several hotel casino properties in Las Vegas and Macau, and turned out to be even better at making money with casinos as he was with trade shows.

Sheldon was and is one tough customer. Nobody tangled with Sheldon and came out on top. I met Sheldon in 2002 when, out of the blue, he called me to see if I wanted to joint venture with him to create a competitor to Comdex, which at the time was owned by a investment vehicle called Key3Media and run by an operator who Sheldon detested. At my meeting in Sheldon's Boston-area office, he related that Fred, Comdex's new owner, had demeaned Sheldon out of jealousy or anger. Fred apparently had all the men's rooms at the Comdex office retitled as "Sheldons." There were other slights too, but mostly Sheldon felt Fred was running Comdex into the ground. And now that Sheldon owned significant event space in Las Vegas, he was ready to go a second round and create a new and better Comdex.

Enter Alan Meckler. Sheldon flattered me by saying that, after his own success, nobody was close to me in knowing how to build and operate a technology trade show. So he proposed that he would put up the funds and give me some equity, and that together we would destroy Comdex.

The first thing he discussed on my arrival at his Boston area and being offered an espresso, was the Sheldons! He went on for three straight hours about his experiences, who he had thought about discussing the new show with, and how he had selected me. By the end of the meeting. I knew he was serious, but was not 100 percent sure about the deal terms and whether Sheldon was committed. The end of the story is that, for a variety of reasons, we did not go forward. I am not just a show operator; I need significant equity to give it my all. Also about this time, another billionaire reached out to me, proposing that I join with his investment group to take over none other than Key3Media, an opportunity that would put me in the saddle to build up Comdex to its former glory. This story requires its own vignette, which follows.

INVEMED, KEN LANGONE, AND SOME OTHER BILLIONAIRES

After the Sheldon Adelson experience, I was surprised and flattered when some other extremely wealthy individuals reached out to me with the proposition that I run not a *competing* Comdex but rather take over the failing owner of Comdex, Key3Media. The acquisition plan called for using significant private equity funds to buy up the sinking bonds that had been used in the formation of Key3Media in order to buy Comdex and some other event properties.

A financier named Michael Solomon, an ex-Lehman Brothers executive from Philadelphia, was given a pot of money to invest on behalf of Ken Langone (who had made billions for organizing the financing for the founders of The Home Depot). Solomon held a series of meetings with me to say that using Langone's Invemed Fund, as well as backing from a financier by the name of Jeff Uben from San Francisco, Mark Lasry of Avenue Fund and some others, I would spearhead running Key3Media, provided his group managed to buy out the bonds and take over Key3Media. I had perhaps six meetings with Solomon and his team, some of which included Ken Langone and Lasry, and I flew out to San Francisco to meet Uben. While I was flattered, I determined the proposed amount of equity for me and my public company was not worth the time and effort. Also, after analyzing the business plan and the numbers, I thought it was overall too risky for the group to take the financial risk. However, after having studied Key3Media and having spent hours with financial people, it occurred to me that one didn't need to buy Key3Media to take out Comdex. Instead, I decided to use my public company at the time, Jupitermedia, to start a new show in Las Vegas at the Mandalay

Bay opposite Comdex on exactly the same days in November 2003. Another vignette is needed to tell the story of ComputerDigitalExpo.

CRAIG NEWMARK

Craigslist is one of the better-known websites in the world. In 1998-99, in my quest to build out my growing website Internet.com, I tried very hard to convince Craig Newmark to sell his ecommerce site to me. In several phone calls with Craig, he was very forthright about his plan to grow Craigslist. At the time, I did not think he could accomplish his plan, but as we now know, Craig was 100 percent correct and I was wrong.

This episode was not dissimilar to my earlier attempt to acquire IMDb.com, the online database devoted to films, TV and videos. At the time, I was being urged by one of my editors, Andrew Kantor, that eyeballs were the key to giant website valuations. IMDb, which had launched in 1990, was certainly one of the larger sites by 1996-97. I thought I was close to making the deal, but then Amazon stepped in and grabbed it.

This was a great fit for Amazon, and less so for Internet.com, but the eyeball factor was, in those days, a great way to increase stock price valuations, and I was watching my company's stock like a hawk. In the end, Craigslist would have been an incredible buy. Much like my almost having a relationship with Yahoo in late 1994-95. Like so many other opportunities, I did not realize at the time how amazingly some of these transactions would have affected the future growth of my business. And yet again, in all cases, the potential sellers perhaps never took my overtures that seriously.

WALL STREET PLAYERS

The 1990s Internet boom and being involved with one of the first Internet IPOs made me a bit of a star. From 1994 to early 2000, I was on CNBC, CNNfn and Bloomberg frequently. But even before the media exposure, I was constantly being called by a variety of Wall Street "players" who wanted to learn about the Internet and how to make money from this new technology.

One of the earliest of these calls came from Bill Gurley, now a general partner at Benchmark, a Silicon Valley venture capital firm in Menlo Park, California. I had breakfast with Bill a few times in 1994 and 1995, as he was learning the Internet basics while at the Wall Street house First Boston.

Another call came from a former top colleague of George Soros: Gerry Manolovicci. Gerry was well known from his Soros days, and he regularly asked me to meet with colleagues to tell them about the Internet and which stocks to buy. I have already mentioned my work with Nancy Peretsman of Allen & Company, the closely-held private investment bank. I probably had lunch at Allen & Co. 30 times or more from 1994 to 1998, where I enjoyed meeting people like Geraldine Leybourne (founder of the Oxygen network).

I realized Nancy and Allen were to a degree using me, but I was getting the Mecklermedia story out into the marketplace, which no doubt helped our stock price. I tended to think I hit it off well with all these people, but I now realize that I was, in fact, just a knowledge asset that would be dropped when no longer useful. Again, this is okay with me because these relationships helped me too.

Over the years, I got to meet many billionaires, including Ken Langone, Sheldon Adelson, Bill Gates, Steve Jobs, Jack Ma, Sam LeFrak and others. Of all of these people, the most interesting in many ways was Sam LeFrak, the real estate tycoon. I had known Sam's son, who recognized in 1996 that I was on to something big with Mecklermedia and the Internet. Soon, his father became interested as well. Sam was a billionaire many times over through real estate holdings in New York City. He became fascinated with the trade show business, and felt it was in many ways similar to real estate, in that the space became valuable and could be sold for more and more at each event. He also mentored me a bit, and would call me every few weeks about the stock price of Mecklermedia — particularly when it slumped. He pumped me up several times by using the real estate metaphor and saying that my assets were solid and not to be bothered by the stock price.

JOHN BACKE

John was introduced to me by two young media bankers by the names of Drew Marcus and Ben Tompkins in 1991. I cannot remember how I met these young fellows, but they loved my early Internet endeavors and thought they might be able to broker a deal with a private equity firm or two that might want to help me grow Internet World.

One of these firms was started by John Backe, who had, among other endeavors, been president of CBS but had lost his job when William Paley pushed him out the door. At the time, Backe was itching to make some waves in media, and so Marcus and Tompkins set up a meeting in a townhouse Backe used as an office on East 52nd Street in Manhattan. Backe had two or three assistants with him. They listened intently to my pitch, as well as my thoughts (or dreams) about where the Internet was headed. We had two or three more meetings, and after one of these I went out to lunch with Drew and Ben at the Bull and Bear restaurant in the old Waldorf Astoria hotel. We really thought a big deal was forthcoming from Backe. But like so many other turndowns, Backe just "did not get the Internet," and I never saw him again. I am sure that within a few years, Backe realized his mistake, like so many other so-called media barons.

DEBATING CRAMER

As the commercial Internet exploded in 1994-95, I became somewhat of a celebrity. This was particularly because of the immense growth of my Internet World properties, but also because I was appearing on CNBC every few weeks to chat about the Internet and my company, Mecklermedia. In those days, there were several "meet-up" events, and one was a breakfast forum produced by Alan Brody. Several times, Brody asked me to be the featured speaker. One of these forums featured me debating CNBC's Jim Cramer and the CEO of TheStreet.com. Our topic was Barnes & Noble versus Amazon.com as a bookseller. Looking back, Cramer aced the debate; he took the position that Amazon would be dominant. My position was that Barnes & Noble would reign supreme because of its vertical focus on books. I was a proponent of vertical focus, and it seemed to me that Barnes & Noble, by concentrating on books as a philosophy, would win out over Amazon's plan to sell books but also start selling other products. Needless to say, I was very wrong.

A GENTLE AUDITOR

Arthur Andersen was one of the great accounting firms in the United States, which was unfairly bankrupted by over-zealous government attorneys in the wake of the Enron scandal. My dealings with this firm came about when I needed an auditor to certify the numbers for Mecklermedia's IPO in 1994. I called the firm out of the blue in my naive way in the fall of 1993, and shortly thereafter Harvey Ganis of the Stamford, Connecticut office called for an appointment. Harvey was career Andersen and was a senior partner. He mentored me and performed services way beyond the obligations of an auditing firm. For example, during the process of going public, when things got tough with the examiner from the SEC, Harvey was always there to tell me not to worry, that he and his team could smooth over any accounting issue. We had a lot of rough patches with the lead lawyer from a prominent Manhattan law firm we used for the IPO. Although Harvey told me that he had never witnessed such shoddy and crass service from a law firm, he nevertheless took the lead to keep the process moving. As an aside, the night before we were to go public, the lead attorney announced he was leaving early to go on a ski trip out West. "No fucking $5 million IPO is going to ruin my ski vacation," he declared. Amazing but true, and I soon dropped that law firm. Alas, Harvey and all his partners got shafted by the Enron scandal. But he was a saint to me during my early public-company days.

THE RICKARD MAN

Perhaps the most interesting business person I ever met was Jack Rickard. A career military man, Jack was an early user and experimenter with what became known as a Bulletin Board System, or a BBS. Bulletin boards were common on the pre-commercial Internet, and were the forerunners of social media. Once you joined a specific bulletin board, you could post your thoughts related to the specialty of that board, and other members could, and would, comment.

I attempted to become the center of this special media area in the 1980s by purchasing a publication called *PLUMB*, created by Ric Manning of Louisville. A tech writer for the Louisville Courier, Manning's passion was BBSs. However, his publication, poorly named *PLUMB*, did not have the funds to grow its circulation before I entered the picture in about 1988. First, I changed the name to *Bulletin Board Systems*; next, I redesigned the publication and published it quarterly.

Like many of my endeavors, BBS (as we called it) floundered. I grew the circulation, from about 150 paid to 700, but there was not enough interest on the part of libraries and others to buy subscriptions to make the title economically successful. Nonetheless, I plugged away at making BBS work. By the time I had started Internet World, I still owned and operated BBS. In fact, the first few drafts of the Mecklermedia IPO included several paragraphs on how our publication, *BBS*, was morphing into a special bulletin board to specifically cover Internet use. Upon reading one of the early IPO draft documents, Chris Locke, whom I had hired in the fall of 1993 to act as my chief advisor for all things Internet, immediately told me that a bulletin board was passé; he said we should change the language to say we were creating one of the first websites in the world that would report on Internet "doings" and more. I remember this as a bolt-from-the-blue moment. Locke's suggestion was the missing link to having vertical and horizontal information about the new Internet industry. Mecklermedia would have dominant trade shows, the dominant magazine and, now, a daily website. Looking back, I imagine our attorneys drafting the IPO documents for the SEC must have thought they were reading science fiction.

So how does this lead into Jack Rickard and ISPCON? Jack, too, had realized electronic bulletin boards were a great pathway to what was becoming a booming business of Internet Service Providers, or ISPs. Remember, in 1993-1994, the only way for a consumer or small business to connect to the fledgling commercial Internet was through a modem connected to a phone line, which in turn connected to the Internet. Another way to connect was via the fast-growing services of America Online or CompuServe, or the smaller Prodigy. Jack recognized that ISPs were going to be the backbone, the middlemen, of the fast-approaching Internet landrush. (There were no browsers, and Netscape's browser wouldn't arrive for another 18 months.)

So, Rickard started a magazine and small event to cover the ISP industry. While my Internet World had immediate explosive growth, starting in 1994, ISPCON took a bit more time to percolate. By 1997, I was looking for another property to grow Mecklermedia even faster. Enter ISPCON and Jack. Jack ran his trade shows like nobody else. Not only did he charge a lot for exhibit space and seminars, he had the audacity to charge around $350 just to *see* the exhibits. In addition, he had a giveaway at each event, usually in the form of a hot vehicle that might have a value in the $30,000 range or more. His shows started to see tremendous growth. I felt the combination of the Internet World and ISPCON was a natural.

Jack ran his operations out of Denver, which is where I met him for the first time, at his office. A beefy fellow with a Texas drawl, who wore a khaki top and bottom, Jack was a gruff, no-nonsense guy. The first thing he told me at the meeting was that CMP Media was in hot pursuit of his company, but that he would rather sell to Mecklermedia because he admired our spunk and loved the public shares. We made a deal quickly, and a few weeks later the acquisition was announced.

Like many maverick entrepreneurs, Jack was not easy to deal with. He had a hard time cooperating, but somehow we managed to control him. (One of our top exhibition-space salesmen moved to Denver from our Westport, Connecticut, office to help with integration.)

But Wall Street did not love the deal, and our stock price dropped from about $28 to $22 after the announcement. Regardless, it was a great deal and ISPCON threw off great cash flow. In time, Jack wanted out and left the business. And a short time after Mecklermedia, was sold to Penton Media. Jack ultimately joined in a class action lawsuit against Mecklermedia, brought by the notorious firm of Milberg Weiss. This legal action was painful to handle and is elaborated upon in another vignette. Nevertheless, I will always remember my dealings with Jack and marvel at how an engineer by training was able to create a dominant trade show at the beginning of the Internet revolution. Ultimately, like many Internet startups, ISPCON would suffer from creative destruction, when the need for ISPs evaporated during the later 1990s, as the browsers took over connectivity. By the same token, the decline of ISPs was also the death knell of America Online, Compuserve, and many related services.

AN EXPENSIVE DOUBLE CROSS

Michael Gartenberg is a very nice fellow and has a great family. He is well known as a tech research analyst and for his work at Apple. My time with him was while he was at Jupiter Research, which I had purchased in 2003.

Mike was the star analyst at Jupiter. We bonded nicely, and he was one of my go-to people for finding out what was happening in the ranks. In 2007, after I sold Jupiter for a tidy profit and had started another enterprise, I came up with the idea that a research business covering rapidly developing mobile apps and related topics would be a winner. But to make it a winner, I needed a top analyst to head the business and help recruit additional analysts. I approached Mike, and he readily agreed to help me start what we were calling Gartenberg Research. We contracted several noted analysts to join us in the launch, and we recruited two former Jupiter sales people. In addition, I had elaborate design work done for the related website. All told, the financial commitment for the launch was $400,000 or more.

All was primed and ready to go, but one problem arose. Mike chickened out! Without Mike, it was a no-go and a big loss, as I had to pay off on guaranteed contracts to sales people, who had quit their jobs, and to analysts, who had asked for guarantees. On one level, I could understand why Gartenberg backed out, perhaps for family reasons and not having the stomach to be an entrepreneur. But after months of work and preparation he took a cowardly path that cost me a lot of money. After this fiasco, whether it be in venture capital investing or in hiring new employees, I always remember cowardly Gartenberg and size up the person I am engaging or investing in, and contemplate if they will be Gartenbergs or lions.

STEVE HARMON AND ISDEX

One of the brightest and best writers who worked with me during the Internet boom in the mid-1990s was Steve Harmon. I first came across Steve when he did research reports for Jupiter Research (several years before I acquired it). Steve went independent, and started writing about Internet stock valuations. I noticed this endeavor, and contacted him about writing under the Mecklermedia umbrella, on our iworld.com site.

While Mary Meeker, then of Morgan Stanley, later became famous for Internet stock analysis, Steve was way ahead of her. I believe he was the first person to conceive of page view valuations. Steve created a universe of public Internet stock valuations, and then started to select those companies he thought were most valuable, based on his own metrics.

This weekly output on iWorld.com was soon offered as an email newsletter, which became hugely popular. Its popularity was behind our spinning off two new commercial products. The first was a $99-a-year subscription to get Steve's stock picks. Within a few weeks of launch, we had over 3000 subscribers! In addition, we created the Internet Stock Index, which we called ISDEX. This, too, became popular. The Kansas City Board of Trade licensed ISDEX, enabling it to trade futures, and Guinness, a large South African mutual fund company, started a mutual fund based on the ISDEX.

In hindsight, "ISDEX" was a bad name for branding. We soon had many imitators, and these competitors used more direct brand names, such as Internet Index. By using "ISDEX," we lost market share to competitors. Also, by 1997, there were at least six or more mutual funds using the term "Internet," and this too hurt our ISDEX brand. Ultimately, there was so much competition that these offerings lost steam. It didn't help that Steve secretly started negotiating with various VC firms to start his own operation, and was eventually backed by a major VC in Silicon Valley. I learned about his leaving by reading about it in *Fortune* magazine! It was quite a shock, but only one of many "loyalty" shocks I faced in my career. Steve ultimately ran into some problems with his business and I lost track of him. While things did not end up great for him — I believe he lost his financial backing — one must credit him with being the first Internet stock analyst pioneer. He was way ahead of Wall Street professionals. And I was pleased that I spotted his talent, and the need to commercialize his writings, before Mary Meeker and many others.

HAL LORD, SUPER SALESMAN

The success of Internet World the trade show was not foreseen. I felt it was a good idea, but then again, from the period between 1971 and 1993, I had countless "good ideas" that ended up losing money, breaking even, or only getting by with a slight profit. However, I was the eternal optimist, always believing that the next idea was going to be a winner.

The December 1994 Internet World trade show at the Washington Hilton in Washington, D.C. was a huge success. We sold out the exhibit space, had over 2000 paid attendees, and total attendance of 5000. During the event, a fellow named Hal Lord appeared in the show office and told me he had built the sales organization for Comdex, the largest tech trade show, at that time, in the world. Readers might not know or remember Comdex. It was created by Sheldon Adelson, who today is one of the wealthiest people in the world, the owner of gambling casinos and real estate in Las Vegas and Macau. Adelson sold his Comdex empire to Masayashi Son of Softbank fame in 1995 for close to $1 billion in cash, and then turned that into countless billions in the casino business. Comdex then is what the Consumer Electronics Show has become: a huge event sprawled over Las Vegas every January. In many respects, however, Comdex was more important than the Consumer Electronics Show because it was the event that helped build the world's computer industry. (Ironically, my Computer Digital Expo, launched in 2003 in Las Vegas, was in many respects the forerunner of the Consumer Electronics Show in that I saw that there would be a blending of the declining Comdex with home devices and electronic games.)

Hal Lord, who had built the methods of selling Comdex for Sheldon Adelson, had recently stopped working for Sheldon. A short and very dapper man of about 50, my first reaction on meeting Hal was that he was a huckster.

But within a few minutes, he had convinced me that if he could spend a few hours with me in my Westport, Connecticut office, he could show me how to turn Internet World into another Comdex-like event.

The meeting in Westport was attended by me and several of my eager lieutenants (all wonderful young women, led by Pamela Burton, who had moved to the U.S. from my London office the year before). We listened to Hal for about an hour. He outlined what we would have to do, which included hiring him and another one of his ex-Comdex colleagues. His biggest idea was that the sales office at the next Internet World in San Jose, California, would have a mammouth floor plan on the wall for the fall 1995 event in Boston. He also recommended that we go back through our records and grade every exhibitor from the three previous Internet World events, giving each points based on exhibit space purchased. We would then assign a number and a time for each of these exhibitors to come to our sales office, during which time they would be given 15 minutes to reserve space, sign a contract and make a down payment of 50 percent of the space cost.

I was a bit incredulous that this would work for our relatively small show on big companies like IBM, Microsoft, Sun Microsystems and others. It wasn't just me. My staff sat there in a state of shock as they listened to Hal's plan. After the presentation, I asked Hal what was in it for him and his colleague. He shot back: $50,000 up front, $100,000 a year, should he prove that the plan worked, *and* stock options.

Hal left for his home outside of Boston. I caucused with my team. We really did not have the funds for such an endeavor, I told them, but then added that I felt Hal was for real. "Let's take a chance that he's on the money," I said.

Much of my career has been built on gut decisions and large gambles. True, many times I have been wrong. But more often, these choices were phenomenally successful, even in my personal life. I got engaged after just a few dates to my wife of 50 years. The same goes for the contemporary art I have purchased after less than a few minutes of viewing or the ocean real estate I bought when it was not in vogue.

Engaging Hal was probably the wisest personnel decision of my career. His concept was expensive, including not only his own fee but the hiring of a full time, ex-Comdex sales manager as our sales manager, a fellow named

Tom Caricini. We also had to have at least six employees from accounting attend the next Internet World, and we had to spend quite a lot on setting up a slick sales office with huge floor-space diagrams, as well as a setup for printing out contracts and taking payments. In addition, the setup included about 30 comfortable chairs where the personnel from prospective exhibitor companies waited for their respective turn to sign up for space at our next show.

The Hal Lord or "Comdex effect" on these waiting people was dramatic. They would see competitors grabbing space, contracting and paying 50 percent deposits. They would also think, while waiting, that if they took *more* space they would be able to move up their selection number for the next show. The model was thrilling to watch. The first time we used it was at the San Jose Convention Center in San Jose, California, where we pre-sold space for Internet World Boston in October 1995. During the three-days of Internet World San Jose (April 1995), we sold nearly 75 percent of the Boston space at the World Trade Center. We were off to the races.

Hal oversaw our sales operations for five years. I now wish we had prepared a video of the saleroom, as it would have served as a great training model for trade shows and related businesses. Sadly, Hal passed away too early, but at least he got to create an incredible success. Hiring Hal when the cost seemed prohibitive was a gamble that paid off 100 fold.

HE HELPED LAUNCH INTERNET WORLD

Ihave related my miserable experience of thinking I had an investor family based in Tulsa, Oklahoma, when I attempted to raise venture funds for my Mecklermedia startup between 1992 and 1993 (Vignette, "Raising Money Disaster"). The folks who told me to come to Tulsa — ostensibly to invest, after deep vetting on the phone, and in New York City, and at my Westport, Connecticut office — asked me to stop in Kansas City on my way to Tulsa to meet with a small trade show services company called Atwood that they owned. This operation was run by a husband and wife team. The business created show directories for large trade shows that were distributed at events around the U.S. The team included sales people who sold ad space in the directories. I will always remember that the husband was "wild" over the old Mobil Gas flying horse logo, and that he had an extensive collection of posters and knick-knacks of the stallion. Overall, I was impressed by their office, business model and some of these sales people I met. Of course, I thought this team was now going to be associated with me, as I was sure the deal would be completed the next day in Tulsa!

Before leaving Kansas City, I made an arrangement for this company to represent my new Internet World trade show because I had no sales team at the time. I figured using freelance sales people would save me money and help grow the show. I was assigned a pleasant young fellow who had just been hired named Chris Fischer. While the Tulsa deal failed, meeting Chris and getting him involved with Internet World was a stroke of good luck.

Although Chris had never sold booth space, he was a natural. Granted, the show topic helped, but Chris was an ace and helped sell out the Washington, D.C., fall Internet World (December 1994). He was so good, I asked him if he would join us full-time, telling him he could remain in Kansas

City if he desired and work out of his apartment. He joined immediately, which was a vote of confidence for our small company. He seemed set in Kansas City. Within three months, however, he moved to our Westport office. And as Internet World's growth accelerated, he soon brought in a good friend of his named Jon Price, also from Kansas City, to help sell the events.

Chis and Jon meshed well with our small team in Westport, and seemed to make several sales every few days. Once Hal Lord (Vignette, "Hal Lord, Super Salesman") came in to take over sales with Tom Caricini, we had a powerhouse sales operation and started adding several people, using the Hal Lord model created at Comdex.

Chris was about the nicest person who ever worked for me. An Iowa native, he left us a few years later to get married and live in Iowa. I kept up with him for a few years. I will never forget his trust, his choice to jump ship in Kansas City and work for me when the future of Internet World was anything but certain. Great fellow.

The lesson here is that luck always plays a big part in business success. I got to meet Chris because of a failed investor meeting. And one needs good employees in order to build.

THE PERSON WHO SOLD
THE FIRST INTERNET AD

It is difficult to believe that there was a time when ads on the Internet or the World Wide Web was thought to be a ridiculous concept.

In 1994, I started one of the commercial Internet's first dozen or so websites. I accomplished this with the help of Chris Locke, who at the time was considered the foremost expert on the concept of websites in the world. It was an exciting time, as those of us in the Internet space knew great things were happening and that explosive change was fast approaching.

About this time, I read about a fellow in Washington, D.C., named Jeff Dearth. Dearth was in charge of marketing and advertising for the New Republic and was dabbling with online advertising. At some point that year, he appeared in major news channels for selling the first Web ad to, I believe, Lufthansa. A few weeks later, Paul Bonnington, one of my employees for Mecklermedia, sold an ad to MCI, the communications company. I think these were the first two ads sold in the Internet space.

Getting back to Dearth.... I happened to meet him at an industry business seminar in Ft. Lauderdale, Florida, in late 1994 or early 1995. We were both invited to be speakers in front of a few hundred media business executives; our topics were related to the future of the Internet and how it would affect traditional magazine and business-to-business publishing.

Jeff and I hit it off immediately. We were both Internet pioneers and true believers. Within days of the meeting, I offered him a job as publisher of my thriving *Internet World* magazine and website called iWorld.com. Jeff accepted and moved his family to Westport, Connecticut.

Jeff was a superb leader and a dynamic sales person. All was great for a few years, but as sometimes happens with such affairs, things can go south.

By the time Jeff joined us, we had launched several print titles too, including *WebWeek*, *WebDeveloper* and the aforementioned *Internet World*. It was a time of rapid development and investment in our iWorld website. It became obvious to me that in order for both the print and website properties to thrive, we had to split the responsibilities and have two publishers, one for the print side of things and another for the website. Jeff did not see it this way, and was hurt that I wanted him to oversee the website operations after I hired a fellow named Dave Egan from McGraw-Hill to be the magazine publisher. Jeff quit, and over the years has been a tremendously successful media banker based in Washington, D.C.

Ironically, I proved to have been right in my decision to split up our operations. I could see, by 1996, that one day all tech publishing of significance would be online, and that the days of large tech print publications were doomed. It did take a few years for me to be proved correct, but it happened. The days were numbered for not only my print titles but those of Ziff-Davis, CMP, IDG and others. Jeff did not see this, and felt the status of being publisher of the largest Internet magazines was far more important than being publisher of iWorld (which later became Internet.com). Further proof is that, after selling Mecklermedia in 1998, Internet.com became a successful public company whose brand exists today. Unfortunately, I believe Jeff always held his leaving the company against me. Fortunately, it worked out well for him, as his media banker business seems to be thriving.

ROBERT KRAKOFF OF ADVANTSTAR

Bob Krakoff was a trade show legend for many years. He passed away a while back, but he was considered, for many years, the top producer of large trade shows worldwide.

I came across Bob in 1997 because my contacts at Chase Bank were also banking for Bob and his company, Advanstar, a huge producer of trade shows around the world. Bob had built the company with an aggressive acquisition strategy. I have mentioned that, starting in 1995, I began getting inquiries about selling Mecklermedia. The fall of 1995 saw Softbank and Masayoshi Son expressing interest, which led to meetings with Ron Fisher of Softbank and his team in Las Vegas in November 1995. Fisher continued the pursuit for at least 18 months, but his offers were always a few dollars per share too low to be considered seriously by the Mecklermedia board. Also during this period, Pat McGovern of IDG kicked the tires at least three times. Once, a deal with IDG seemed imminent. With Nancy Peretsman of Allen and Company acting as the broker — I believe it was around Memorial Day, 1996 — I was ready to take the deal to my board. But Pat, as usual, changed the deal terms so that much of the cash was taken off the board, and the deal died. Pat had this habit of talking big numbers, but then when the paperwork arrived, the cash part of the deal had been changed to a complicated barter.

A few months later, after the Memorial Day deal fell apart, my angel investor Jim Mulholland, Jr. Got me and Pat together at his New York City apartment overlooking Central Park. The goal was to make yet another deal. Jim had known Pat for many years, and they were good friends. It seemed certain we had another deal, one that might get to fruition. But Pat once again changed the terms dramatically.

Krakoff, on the other hand, was all business when I met him in 1997 at Chase headquarters on Park Avenue in New York City. Like many media moguls, Krakoff had an imperial manner and got right to the point. He was there to buy Mecklermedia. He said he had studied our public numbers, and then, amazingly, told me that all he wanted was the weekly *Internet World* magazine and the trade shows by the same name. He did "not want to touch" the website. His offer was $210 million — and he did not want to negotiate. Being a public company, if we'd accepted such an offer, we would have had to figure out what to do with the website asset, but I did not have to spend too much time pondering this dilemma because our board rejected Krakoff's offer.

Interestingly, in the next few months, offers would come in from United Business Media in London and Penton Media in Cleveland, Ohio. These were sophisticated business media companies, and like Bob Krakoff, neither wanted much to do with the Internet.com website.

Because Bob Krakoff brought up the issue, I started to think of how to handle a sale of Mecklermedia that did not include this website. When the time came to make such a deal, I was mentally prepared to discuss such an offer.

The take-away from the Krakoff discussion was that, even though the Web had been around since 1993, and large investments were being made and large valuations were commonplace, sophisticated media barons were still reluctant to buy the idea that websites were here to stay and that their valuations would skyrocket down the road. I had already seen the light (witness my cutting back on print publishing in 1996). Several of my competitors at ZiffDavis and CMP said I was "cutting and running" because I could not figure out the print business. But it was just the opposite. I was years ahead of everybody. I had figured out the future before anybody else, much as I had "seen" the Internet years before others.

KEYNOTER STORIES

We had an incredible line up of keynote speakers at our various Internet World events in the U.S. By 1997, we were producing annual events in New York, at the Javits Center, in Chicago, at the McCormick Center, and in Los Angeles, at the Los Angeles Convention Center. We routinely attracted 60,000-plus attendees at all three events, as well as 3,000 or more paid seminar attendees, and would make upwards of $5 million or more per event. Generally, we had five keynotes spread over three days. An array of tech company all-stars were selected for these slots. The premiere spot was the opening keynote. Depending on the size of the keynote auditorium, we would seat 3,000 to 6,000 people. I opened the events with a brief welcome speech, and then would introduce the keynoter.

Here's a list of some of our notable keynoters:

- Eric Schmidt (then of Novell, after many years at Sun Microsystems)
- Larry Ellison (Oracle)
- Lou Gerstner (IBM)
- Gil Amelio (Apple, and one of the CEOs during the Steve Jobs banishment)
- Michael Dell (Dell Computer)
- Jerry Yang (Yahoo)
- Jim Barksdale (Netscape)
- Bill Joy, and later, Ed Zander (Sun Microsystems)
- Steve Case (AOL)
- Steve Jobs (Next Computer)
- Bill Gates (Microsoft)

And there were countless others, from now-forgotten organizations like Real Networks and Borland.

By 1998, we were producing Internet World events in at least 10 countries. I attended every show; our keynoters in these international locations were generally top executives from that country or the local general manager of the likes of IBM or some other international tech giant.

While I did not spend much time with the keynoters before introducing them, there are some interesting memories from these brief encounters. Lou Gerstner, then chairman of the board and CEO of IBM, had significant security with him, preventing me from having any interaction with him. Larry Ellison, co-founder of Oracle, refused to enter the stage from the "green room" or off stage, but rather insisted on walking down the center aisle of the Javits keynote auditorium with several of his aides accompanying him. It was agreed beforehand that once he came up onto the stage after my introduction, he would shake my hand and commence his presentation. When he came up the stairs, I walked over to him to shake hands. He presented a very strong grip and nearly threw me aside! Fortunately, I caught my balance and doubt many in the audience noticed the awkwardness. Michael Dell, founder and CEO of Dell Technologies, seemed very down to earth, as did Steve Jobs; both exchanged pleasantries with me prior to the start of the conference. I remember Gil Amelio and his Apple handlers insisted that I read a lengthy and quite boring preamble on a teleprompter for his introduction. The introduction was laborious, and so I decided to go off script. The Apple handlers who controlled the teleprompter scrolling before me went crazy, and started highlighting what I was skipping. Knowing Amelio was on his way out, I was not too concerned about the consequences of my editing. Bill Gates, who I knew slightly, decided not to present in person, but instead had a broadcast hook-up for his presentation. (The reason? His wife was about to give birth.) It would have been interesting to see Gates in person because, by then (April, 1996), he had gotten steamed at me for reminding him in 1995 about my earlier meeting with him in 1993 when we first discussed the future of the Internet. I recall he clearly "did not get it," as far as I was concerned, as he extolled the virtues of the CD-ROM. At the time, it was certain to me that the CD-ROM was dead, and that the Internet was the future (this was also about the time I sold my CD-ROM World magazine and related assets to Pat McGovern of IDG). Eric Schmidt, who would later become a multi-billion-aire from mentoring the Google founders, was at the time of his keynote, in the summer of 1996 in Chicago, very appreciative of our selecting him to be the opening keynoter of the first summer Internet World. The last time I saw Schmidt, at a small event at the Puck Building in New York City about the future paid search, was just after he had been appointed to his Google position. Nobody at that time could have possibly thought Google would become the mega-powerhouse of today, but Eric reminisced about the Internet World days and again expressed his appreciation of being our keynoter. He had just taken over as CEO of Novell after having been CTO at Sun Microsystems for many years.

WOULDA, COULDA, SHOULDA

Dealing with Ziff Davis and its various CEOs was frequent for me from 1991 to 1995. I have related about my meetings with Philip Korsant in 1992, when he was, as many were, clueless about the Internet. Next, I had several encounters with Eric Hippeau, starting in 1992, and Scott Briggs, and they too were clueless too. But by 1994, Eric had gotten the message that the Internet was for real.

Eric has become incredibly successful as the original CEO of HuffPost, and then as a venture capitalist, first with Masayoshi Son, the Japanese billionaire businessman who serves as chairman and chief executive officer of Japanese holding company SoftBank, and then with Lerer Hippeau, the seed stage VC fund.

It is shocking to think that someone who has made so much money in and around the Internet was clueless about it in 1992-93. But some smart people figure things out, and Eric is brilliant. Another ZD alum was Herschel Sarbin, who had taken over Cowles Business Media by 1992. Herschel, too, just could not get his arms around the Internet concept, and walked away from an incredible sweetheart deal that would have made Cowles a powerhouse in tech media.

Another fellow who has made huge amounts of money in and around the Internet is Alan Patricof, now chairman emeritus of Greycroft Ventures. If one reads Michael Wolff's book "Burn Rate," one will find a hilarious story that Wolff relates about Patricof not understanding the Internet in 1992. Wolff today is known as a best-selling author for his books on Donald Trump, but the man was one of the first entrepreneurs in the Internet space with his so-called NetGuides, which were booklets that listed interesting websites in a variety of subjects.

This brings me to Dan Rosensweig, who became head of ZiffDavis online in 1999 when it was spun out from the print business, ZiffDavis Media. Dan was a pleasant fellow whom I met initially at a Piper Jaffray Internet conference in Minneapolis in 1996. Dan later merged Ziff Davis Online into CNET, and then went on to make a fortune as the No. 2 executive at Yahoo, when it was resurrected in the later 1990s under (Terry Semel, a former Hollywood producer). Dan recognized that his stock was floundering and that my public company, Internet.com, was a natural choice to merge with. (This would surely titillate Wall Street and day traders, who were speculating wildly on Internet stocks.) I met several times with Dan about a merger, and we came close. But in the end, Dan wanted to be CEO and I felt I was the better person to head the combined operations, since I was on CNBC and CNNfn quite often, while Dan had no public persona. Looking back, it probably made sense to merge, but as I have stated in this book numerous times, I had many critical decisions to make "on the fly," and not all of them were, in hindsight, for the best. Also, whether it was Dan or others who approached me about deals in these years, we were all affected by thinking that our stock prices could only go higher and higher. Few of us were as smart as Mark Cuban, who placed collar hedges on his shares to ensure that a billion dollar cash net worth would be safe if the Internet mania went sour. For Dan, things only got better. He landed at Yahoo when few realized Yahoo would be doomed by the coming of Google. But this was a few years off, and Dan made out very well, becoming quite a popular celebrity in tech circles. Good for Dan.

INTERNET HOTSHOT

The go-go years of the Internet IPO boom will probably never happen again. Today we have unicorns whose valuations are vastly larger than the typical IPO of the 1990s, but we had companies going public back then based on an idea, venture capital, and something called "barter revenue."

Barter was a simple concept that took Wall Street by storm. Company A gave ad space to Company B, and B did the same with A. Both declared that the ad space was worth "X" dollars, and so barter revenue was born. EarthWeb, a company that I had many dealings with, was a prime example: it went public and achieved close to a billion dollar market cap on its first day of trading, mostly on "earnings" from barter revenue. There were critics of this practice, for sure, but nothing could hold back the Internet IPO craze, and barter revenue gave these startups the aura and gravitas they needed to satisfy the SEC, Wall Street bankers, and speculators.

One fellow who knew how to play this better than anyone was Russ Horowitz of Seattle, Washington. When I first met Russ in the mid-1990s, he was already very IPO wealthy (on paper) from his high flyer Go2Net stock holdings. Russ was a handsome fellow with blonde curly hair and a big toothy smile. When he walked into a room, you felt he was your friend. He knew this for sure, and parlayed it into making lots of deals. Overall, he was very capable and smart, in addition to being well-connected. After we were introduced by an investment banker, Russ visited my New York City office on East 42nd Street, near Madison Avenue. We hit it off so well that we started talking about merging our operations. Go2Net offered services to help online businesses and offline businesses reach more customers. Much like with many offers I had back then to merge, I loathed the idea of not being CEO. I also suffered the problem of always thinking my stock was undervalued, and could only become more valuable in my quest to become a billionaire. I remained business friendly with Russ, and would see him on his frequent journeys to Manhattan. Then, one day, I read about his pulling off a great coup: he got Paul Allen to put in a $60 million or more as a private placement into Go2Net. Not only was this amazing sum, but Paul Allen, a co-founder of Microsoft, gave Russ a validation that few of us had. Go2Net stock's must have jumped 100 points that day (it was not uncommon in the mid-1990s to 2000 for Internet stocks to have swings of 30 points, or huge percentage gains or drops daily). I realized then and there that maybe I should have done the merger with Russ. Frankly, I don't remember exactly what happened to Russ and Go2Net after the Internet crash in April of 2000, but I am sure he was one of the smart ones who used a collar/hedge to lock in his millions.

Looking back, Russ was one of probably 30 entrepreneurs that I became business friendly with during the Internet go-go years. It was an incredible time to pal around with these fellows, as all of us were worth hundreds of millions or billions. And it seemed this would go on forever. The big difference for me was that I was long in the tooth compared to my Internet pals. By this time, I was 51 or so, while most of these new friends were in their mid-to-late 20s. I could relate to them on many levels, but on one level — experience — I felt a bit superior. I did recognize that they were all very smart, and many were even dashing like Russ or Mark Cuban (whom I met in 1995). Deep down, I wondered what they thought of me, but I did not dwell on this topic as there were millions and maybe billions to be made from the deals and opportunities that were flowing to me daily.

TWO WHO BAILED ME OUT

I have written how, in the years between 1975 and 1999, I too often launched fledgling publications without considering cash flow. I found it difficult to turn down what I considered to be a great idea. Also, the type of publishing I was doing at the time lent itself to rapid launches, provided I had a good idea and could find an expert editor or writer to create content on a timely basis. I was also blessed with an incredible editor-in-chief named Tony Abbott, who never balked at a new launch and always performed to keep publications on schedule. Most of these launches were critically well received. They were not necessarily cash flow positive, but the nature of research library publishing was that the publisher got paid in advance annually, through subscription agents and libraries.

While it was great to get this cash upfront, I usually had cash flow problems because I had too many of these specialty periodicals that needed to be promoted and produced. During the period between 1980 and 1990, there would be several times each year when I was cash short and had to sweat making payroll. I was fortunate that two different publishing companies were willing, on short notice, to purchase a publication, which I had put up for sale in order to raise badly needed cash.

The first of these publishers was Bob Hagelstein, president of Greenwood Press, just down the road from my Meckler Publishing offices in Westport, Connecticut. I met Bob while working at Greenwood from 1971 to 1972, and we bonded. Bob had worked his way up to become president of Greenwood, which was a large scholarly publisher producing several hundred new books annually. Bob knew my product line, kept up with my ideas, and was aware of most of my publications' critical successes. I could call him up and say, "I need to raise $25,000 or so, and I know you think highly of such and such publication. For $25,000 or so, you can take it over, including the subscription liability," which pertained to the yet-to-be published issues of a subscription that a library had pre-paid for.

A deal could be completed within a week, as we were both experts at writing quick purchase agreements. With this deal done, perhaps a few months later I would be offering Bob a reference book collection or another scholarly newsletter or journal.

My other great resource in those days was Charles Chadwyck-Healey, who was based in Cambridge, England. Charles was perhaps the most erudite professional I dealt with in my career, and also the most capable. His forte was large research collections published on microfilm or microfiche that might sell for as much as $50,000 or more. An example would be "The Papers of Parliament" or some similar, important collection that would take years to assemble, edit and film. One Chadwyck-Healey bailout was his agreeing to purchase all of Meckler Publishing's botanical collections on microfiche, which were in the midst of production, including some joint venture projects with Charles. I happened to be in England on a business trip, and knew that in less than a month it was likely I would not be able to make payroll and pay several large bills. At this point in the mid-1980s, I had known Charles for 15 years and had worked closely with him and his staff. I visited his office and laid out my dilemma. Within two hours, we had a deal, and a check was written for close to $50,000, even before the paperwork was completed.

Although I was always saddened to have to sell some of my projects, necessity called for such action. It took me many years to "sober up" and realize I needed to focus on technology publishing, so I could get out from under my cash flow problems. Looking back, I see how blessed I was to have relationships with people like Bob and Charles. I also realize that, even today, I have to restrain myself from jumping at publishing something (today it would be creating a website) when a good idea pops into my head. It took me years to curtail my weakness to continually pump out publications. I have a fondness for many of my publication ideas, many of which exist today under the ownership of other organizations.

The advice I have for an entrepreneur reading this vignette is to remember that every expansion of a business model in another direction can have dire cash flow implications for the future of a business. Therefore, before launching any new activity make sure cash flows are projected for worst-case scenarios and do not fall in love with the new idea.

PERSONALITIES WORTH MENTIONING

While most of my history is associated with media or tech types, it is worth mentioning some other personalities I have come across during my career.

Take Robert F. Kennedy. I had an incredible time working in his New York senatorial office from 1965 to 1967. I was hired as an intern from a program attached to Columbia College, which I attended at the time. This was after the JFK assassination and was perhaps the height of Kennedy mania. I would spend several hours a week in the New York office above the United States Post Office building on 45th Street near Lexington Avenue. My tasks ranged from the mundane to the somewhat meaningful. My main job was to answer telegram requests as though I was RFK. Every day there would be requests coming in for the Senator to attend an event, ranging from a wedding to a town meeting, from all over New York State. I probably wrote 30 or more replies a week, and always signed them " Robert Kennedy." In addition, I would get assignments to escort out of town dignitaries, such as governors or senators, around New York City, including picking them up at LaGuardia Airport. I also worked as an advance man for the Senator in and around New York City. This entailed appearing at a function several minutes to hours before the Senator arrived to give a speech. My job, with others, was to make sure everything was in order, such as AV, seating and other necessities. My biggest task in this area was to help run public forums for the 1966 gubernatorial primary across New York City and the State. It was an interesting group that includedFranklin D. Roosevelt Jr., Howard Samuels, Paul O'Dwyer and Frank O'Connor. One time, I was asked to volunteer for John V. Lindsay's mayoral campaign in New York City, and to essentially spy on what I saw, including bringing back to the office policy papers and literature. The biggest thrill was delivering a portable TV set to Jacqueline Kennedy's apartment on the Upper East Side and getting a glimpse of the former first lady.

I also spent time at the United Nations interviewing staff from Latin American countries prior to the Senator's trip to South America.

My grandest memory is from 1966, when senior staff asked me to bring several friends from Columbia to the Senator's apartment at the United Nations Plaza on the East River of Manhattan to discuss the draft. The Senator felt that the draft, or conscription, was in many ways was unfair to minorities and wanted to get our viewpoints. I had previously had brief interactions with RFK at the New York office but never for more than a minute at a time. This meeting was special. The Senator offered us drinks. I remember him taking his scotch on the rocks and using his index finger to stir the contents — to this day, I remember this every time I have a drink. We spent about two hours with the Senator and his aide Tom Johnston talking about Vietnam and the draft. I still remember looking out on the East River and seeing the large Pepsi Cola neon sign across the river in Long Island City.

I now happen to live in Manhattan, where I have a view of this very sign. Every day I see it, and it always takes me back to spending two hours with RFK at his New York City apartment.

When RFK ran for president in 1968, I was asked to be an advance man for the campaign. But I had to decline, since taking the position would have resulted in my being drafted for the Vietnam War. (I had a deferment that year to obtain a master's degree at Columbia.)

At the time RFK was assassinated in Los Angeles on June 6, 1968, I was in the midst of awaiting orders to become part of the U.S. Army Intelligence, as a second lieutenant. I had time on my hands awaiting a security clearance, so I could begin my training at Fort Holabird, Maryland. I was shocked, but remembered how at rallies around New York City the Senator was pawed at, and how his aides would stand behind him and hold him by his back pant pockets. I was most affected by the service at St. Patrick's Cathedral in New York City, and then watching the train ride on television from New York to Washington, D.C.

Not to be compared to these RFK memories were my interactions with long-time-retired crooner Rudy Vallée in 1970, when I worked at Kennikat

Press, which was reprinting his autobiography. Another interesting interaction was a lunch with former head of the CIA William Colby. I had Colby give a keynote address at a conference I was producing at the New York Hilton on CD-ROM. He had recently been associated with an "action" CD-ROM game, and his keynote recounted his being behind enemy lines in Germany during World War II. We had a fascinating, two-hour lunch with some of my editorial staff.

I had some dealings with the journalist Carl Bernstein, who was involved with a startup in 2004. He was incredibly persistent, to the point of annoyance. I remember one time being in Venice, Italy, on vacation when Carl wanted my input and investment on a project. I had no interest, but he would not give up calling me until, finally, my wife picked up the mobile phone and asked him to stop calling. I guess his persistence was part of being an investigative reporter, but it was not pleasant being on the receiving end of his calls.

I had the pleasure of spending time with the publisher of *The New York Times*, Arthur Sulzberger, along with his good friend Sidney Gruson, and the actor, singer and comedian Zero Mostel. The occasion was two dinners aboard the Queen Elizabeth 2 crossing the Atlantic in the summer of 1977. My mother-in-law and my wife were with me on the crossing, and she got us invited to the dinners on two consecutive nights. All these men were fascinating. I remember waiting for Mostel to be funny, but of course he was not on stage.

While writing my Ph.D. dissertation and other research projects, I spent time with the original head of the Selective Service System, Lewis Hershey. I also interviewed Albert Boni, creator of the paperback book as we know it today when he owned a company called Boni and Liveright in the 1920s. Another interview subject was Hamilton Fish II, one of the staunchest isolationists leading up to World War II.

The most flamboyant personality I met was the painter LeRoy Neiman. I met Neiman, before he was famous, while at Columbia in the 1960s. I have always had an interest in art and spent many hours with LeRoy at his most-interesting studio in Manhattan. He lived in the Hotel des Artistes near Lincoln Center in an amazing apartment whose living room ceiling was about 16 feet high. LeRoy was known for sports art with lots of color. I had no money to buy his art, but he did autograph for me the cover of *Time* that featured his painting of Jets quarterback Joe Namath.

I also got to spend time with close Kennedy family associate Kenneth O'Donnell during my work with RFK. I spent several hours with him one night while attending to Senator Gaylord Nelson of Wisconsin at a party in New York City. I never asked about JFK, but he probed my interest in conscription and wanted to know about my studies and interests. It was a most memorable evening. Senator Ted Kennedy got so drunk that he had to be carried out by O'Donnell and other Kennedy associates from a Park Avenue townhouse owned by a publisher.

I could go on and write about the many not-so-famous individuals I met, worked with, or interviewed in over 50 years of being an entrepreneur. These people are not "famous," but many were extremely interesting.

DEALS/ NEGOTIATION

PHOTOS.COM,
THE MICROSTOCK REVOLUTION
AND BLOWING A BILLION DOLLARS

My career has taken me in many directions. I played a hunch in 2002 that entering the online stock photo business could be a winner.

At the time, my public company was called INTMedia. We had a website called Internet.com with close to 30 million unique visitors that made money from selling ad space. We also had a growing trade show called Search Engine Strategies, which had its own companion websites. But I did not believe that Internet.com, our newest domain, would demonstrate significant growth to interest Wall Street in our stock, which was selling at about $2.00 a share, after the Internet stock crash of April 2000.

One of my lieutenants, Dave Arganbright, suggested we consider purchasing a small company in Tucson, Arizona, called Photos.com. It had a few million dollars in revenue, was profitable and was growing rapidly. We purchased the business in 2002 for $17 million in cash, plus a bit of our publicly traded stock.

The genius of Photos.com was that it sold inexpensive stock photos by subscription. Although not the highest quality images, the model was great for advertising agencies and online sites that needed lots of imagery but did not want to pay the top dollar charged by the likes of Getty Images and Corbis.

The man behind Photos.com was Peter Garepy. Garepy had realized that creative destruction could take place in the lucrative field of stock photos. Getty Images was a Wall Street darling because it charged a lot for a royalty-free photo that it could sell over and over again. Garepy, however, understood that a subscription plan of about $99.00 a month, giving the purchaser unlimited photos, was a winning formula.

Within months of the purchase, our public stock started to rise. In between, we also purchased Jupiter Research, a research company specializing in research related to all business aspects of the Internet that had launched in 1994. Jupiter, had been valued at close to $1 billion as a public company in late 1999, was about to declare bankruptcy for about $200,000. (More about Jupiter Research later.)

After the Jupiter deal, we changed the name of the public company to Jupitermedia. It had an images division (Jupiterimages), an online media division (Internet.com) and search engine trade shows. But Wall Street was only enamored with Jupiterimages.

Photos.com was a money machine. Within 6 months of the acquisition, our stock had tripled. This sparked my appetite for purchasing more stock photo companies. That was a terrible mistake, but it took several years for me to see I had taken the wrong fork in the road. The brilliance of Photos.com was its pricing, and the insatiable appetite of hundreds of thousands commercial and consumer users who wanted inexpensive stock photos.

Mistake No. 2 was my not understanding another brilliant Garepy idea: bypass "professional" photographers whose photos were being purchased to sell on Photos.com and, instead, invite amateurs to send in photos for possible sale. These photos could then be offered for as little as $1 or less. This new pool of photos was limitless, particularly after the launch of the the iPhone in June 2007. This smartphone and the others that followed it allowed anyone to shoot photos rapidly and for no expense.

Garepy called his new idea "Rebel Artist." Unfortunately, I did not see the brilliance of Rebel Artist and what it could bring: a huge way to grow operations for little cost by going even more "down market" than Photos.com.

On a trip to Tucson, I told Garepy to shut down Rebel Artist and to concentrate on growing the Photos.com model. I told him that we would also go out and purchase several small, but important, traditional stock photo companies. Garepy was so pleased with what was happening with the growth of Photos.com that he did not protest my decision.

In hindsight, this was a several-billion-dollar mistake and one I think about at least every few weeks.

Interestingly, about the time we shut down Rebel Artist, a team in Calgary, Canada, started a business similar to Rebel Artist called iStockPhoto. This business was offered to me in 2005 for $5 million. One of my photo lieutenants, Patty Vargas, told me to grab it. Instead, I listened to my financial team, who thought a company with $300,000 annual revenue (but growing at over 100 percent every 6 months) was a stupid purchase. Concentrate on the Photos.com model and keep buying upscale stock photo companies, they told me.

I remember clearly standing in my CFO's office with my gut saying we should buy iStock now. But I went against my gut feeling — a decision that has haunted me for years.

In late 2005, I realized the mistake I had made and offered $15 million for 49 percent of iStock. But during these negotiations, Getty Images jumped in and bought the whole operation for $50 million.

The irony is that Jonathan Klein, a founder and CEO of Getty Images, had been telling Wall Street for years that Photos.com was a "crap image" model and that quality was what counted. But he wised up and grabbed iStock to fight off the coming revolution in stock images, a decision that ultimately saved Getty Images.

We went on to purchase a 49 percent interest in a Hungarian start-up called Stockxpert that had the same model as iStockPhoto, and was likewise having great growth. Unfortunately, the young founder was too headstrong to listen to how best to grow the business and compete with Getty, and so a great opportunity was lost for Jupiterimages.

The last part of the saga is Jon Oringer and his startup called Shutterstock. Oringer was a young entrepreneur who also understood that the iStock model could raise havoc on the traditional stock photo business model. His wrinkle over iStockPhoto and Stockxpert was to use the subscription model that had been fostered by our Photos.com. But he melded the Photos.com subscription model with the iStock concept, which proved to be the best formula, and made him a billionaire.

Oringer approached me several times in 2005 about having Jupiterimages purchase an interest in Shutterstock. He wanted $5 million for a 49 percent share. Once again, I whiffed. I turned him down and bet on

Stockxpert, even though I was having trouble controlling the founder of Stockxpert. A few years later, Oringer returned and offered 20 percent for $19 million. We turned him down again. The private equity firm Insight took the deal with Oringer, and Shutterstock became a huge success. It went public in 2012, and today has a valuation in the billions.

I was right about the future of stock photos online. But I made some bonehead decisions — more later on those, and my bad luck — and it personally cost me hundreds of millions, not to mention that the financial crisis of 2008 that made things worse for Jupiterimages.

THE MEDIABISTRO AND
SOCIAL MEDIA VENTURE YEARS

In 2007, I purchased Mediabistro, a resource for media professionals, for $20 million in cash. The seller was the mercurial Laurel Touby and her partners. Several colleagues warned me not to make the purchase, but I felt the Mediabistro community, database, and other assets would make it a great foundation on which to build a trade show and an online learning company.

The deal was $20 million down, plus a chance for the sellers to gain an additional $3 million in earn outs (in the end, only about $750,000 was earned). Touby had built an interesting platform that originally catered to the publishing, editorial and writing community. The Mediabistro online job board was second to none in serving this community, particularly in New York City, Boston, Washington, D.C. and San Francisco down to Los Angeles. When I made the purchase, the job board was growing rapidly and was getting hundreds of new job postings weekly. Growth was well over 30 percent annually. Also, Mediabistro had started an online learning business that was thriving off a physical, evening class model first launched in 2001.

The database was impressive, with hundreds of thousands names. In fact, Mediabistro had everything but a trade show operation. I saw all the assets in front of me and figured that I would add events, expanding this event business into a major business-to-business company.

Feeling that online learning had a huge upside, I approached a company called Linda.com in the hope of merging or purchasing the property to help jumpstart Mediabistro's online learning program. However, Linda.com's owner wisely turned me down. Several years later, management was able to sell Linda.com to LinkedIn for close to a billion dollars.

And, unfortunately, several events occurred in rapid succession that all but destroyed my dreams of building a great media company.

The aforementioned Linkedin had added a job board, as had several other online services, including Indeed.com.

Next, and most importantly, came the financial crisis of 2008. Once this hit, our job board went from over 1000 new postings a week to a low of a few hundred listings—a condition from which the Mediabistro job board never recovered (and why the sellers never got much of an earn out). The job board had been a cash-cow business for us, but the cash flow evaporated with the financial crisis, coupled with the competitive onslaught from Linkedin.

We did launch several events, but by 2010 I knew that Mediabistro was in a slow death spiral. Eventually, I was able to sell most of the Mediabistro assets for $8 million in cash to a division of Prometheus Media, which ultimately failed to thrive.

The Mediabistro years included my swinging for the fences by buying several social media blogs and related products as the infant social media field was exploding. The idea was to become the center of the social media business world with daily news, events and research, and strap these assets onto the base of Mediabistro.

My first move was to attempt to purchase Mashable, what was considered at the time the No. 1 blog in the social media space. Mashable had been created a year or so earlier by a 23-year-old Scot by the name of Pete Cashmore. In 2009, I worked out a deal to buy Mashable from him for $11 million cash, giving him a chance to earn double that over a several-year period, based on performance thresholds. We had the contracts completed, but while we were waiting for Cashmore to sign, he pulled out of the deal. I was disappointed for sure. But what was most shocking was the way Cashmore handled the cancelation. No explanation, no apology, no nothing. Cashmore ultimately sold Mashable for a fraction of what he thought he would garner, as he'd essentially destroyed a valuable property by getting what I called at the time "Huffington Post envy." Cashmore had a great social media site, but he craved to be bigger and tried to cover everything from culture to politics. I have made a lot of mistakes in my career, but I never treated a buyer or seller in the nasty way Cashmore treated me.

In late 2009 and on the rebound, we bought Allfacebook.com from a very young smart fellow named Nick O'Neill. Nick was based in Washington, D.C., and latched on to the idea several years earlier that Facebook would be very big and that he would cover it "every which way." To that end, Nick started an event series dealing with social media development. It was a nice little business. His competitor in the space was a fellow named Justin Smith, who at about the same time launched Inside Social Networks and a blog called InsideFacebook.com, which included a research property called AppData. Smith also had an event by the name of Inside Social Apps. We bought these properties as well. We also bought, from a brilliant San Francisco entrepreneur named Charles Hudson, a group of small events with brands such as Virtual Good Summit, Freemium Summit and more. Within 18 months, I had amassed a conglomeration of social media properties second to none and figured that while the Mediabistro core was somewhat worthless, I could roll in social media to its infrastructure and still create a powerful business-to-business media company.

The deal seemed brilliant. The Inside Social Apps show, which had 1000 paid seminar attendees and about 50 exhibitors in February 2011, seemed to be on a trajectory to become a major trade show. The AppData product was equally strong, and was tripling in sales and customers every six months. But it all went wrong by 2013.

First, we lost all of Smith's key writers, including Editor in Chief Eric Eldon and Business Development Chief Susan Su. It turned out that these two were the glue that made the whole operation thrive. Next, AppData was hurt severely when Facebook shut us out from getting certain data related to the many apps that were being launched by app developers worldwide. Losing this data was the death knell for our product. The final nail in the coffin was that the whole basis for a social app show died. It turned out that once a developer learned the basics of app development, there was nothing much more to learn, making a $600 seminar fee no longer a necessity. So the show died.

I found it hard to watch all of these events, but I had been tempered over the years by lots of failures (along with successes), so I gulped and started looking for the next big thing.

Looking back, I was more bothered by the nastiness, meanness, immorality and, most of all, the lack of honesty by several 20-somethings that worked for me or who came along with the acquisitions. Nick O'Neill was a stalwart, but most of the people from Inside Social Networks were downright ingrates and immoral. One person in particular, a writer, had the gall to attend a German event I was running in Berlin called AllFacebook.com. She insisted on business class. She came to Berlin and did some interviews, but never came to the event or stopped by to say hello to the staff or to me. She never apologized because, in her mind, this was normal, entitled behavior.

DAILY CANDY

One of the more hilarious of my VC deals involved a young woman named Dani Levy. Based in New York City, Levy was the creator of a slick daily email newsletter called The Daily Candy, which covered fashion, food and other topics that would appeal to young women in New York City.

The year was 1999, just about the height of Internet start-up investment and valuations. Dani was actually a friend of one of my daughters, so it was a breezy and friendly first meeting about raising funds for her start-up. I met with her at my Fifth Avenue office, across from the main branch of New York Public Library, and had a few of my young assistants along for the meeting.

I saw great upside in what was being offered, as I envisioned having many versions of the newsletter for different U.S. cities and, ultimately, world cities. The valuation, as I remember it, was not insignificant. While sitting there, I offered about $100,000 for 10 percent of the business. Dani tentatively agreed. We thought we had a deal.

But a few days later, while waiting for her documents, she called to apologize, offering a unique story as her excuse to withdraw from the deal. It seems that Dani had *already* made deals to sell more than 100 percent of The Daily Candy. She said she had to somehow unwind herself from the mess. I hoped we would hear from her again, but we did not. A few years later, she sold her business for a good many millions to a large media company. The consolation was that my original instinct about the upside had been correct.

EARTHWEB

The go-go days of Internet IPOs ran from 1995 to the spring of 2000. I believe there were about 230 IPOs listed in the article in *Barron's* in late March of 2000 by Jack Willoughby on burn rates that started the Internet stock crash of 2000-2003. My company at the time, Internet.com, was one of only 10 in the article that had positive cash flow. Yet, when the crash came, our stock was pummeled from about $60 a share to the low single digits. It was very painful.

Before the crash, many Internet companies went public with no revenue other than what was known as "barter" revenue. Barter revenue was based on the swapping of ad space between or among other Internet companies, each of whom counted the space swap as ad revenue.

Perhaps the best example of this shenanigan was a company called EarthWeb, which went public in the late 1990s with a market cap of several hundred million dollars in its first day of trading. EarthWeb's founders were two good showmen: brothers Jack and Murray Hidary. Wall Street loved them—particularly Jack. In fact, after the death of his Internet company, Jack had the chutzpah to run for mayor of New York City.

In fairness, EarthWeb had some serious developer content and some great ideas. Unfortunately, it had little to no real-dollar revenue. So when the crash came, it was in big financial trouble. But EarthWeb's financial trouble was music to my ears because my company, though slaughtered on its stock price, was sitting with a great cash position. Unlike them, we had a great business and made money. Seeing a good opportunity (much like the purchase of Jupiter Research), I contacted the Hidarys about an acquisition. At the time, this was probably seen as shocking, since I had been vocal in the press about EarthWeb's accounting. (Some saw my criticism as jealousy, but

I was just speaking the truth.) But I knew EarthWeb had great content and felt I had to have it for Internet.com.

I remember going to the EarthWeb offices, which occupied several high floors at Park Avenue South, and had incredible views in several directions. The EarthWeb offices had all kinds of cool spaces, something that was expected of Internet companies back then. They had workout rooms and even a piano. Regardless, my meeting with my team and the key EarthWeb management was short and sweet. See, nobody wanted EarthWeb but me. My offer? The whole operation for the assumption of its liabilities. Within 10 minutes we had a deal. I remember Murray had a bit of a fit at my offer, but swallowed the deal on the condition that we would not publicly discuss the rapidity of the deal nor gloat that we had purchased EarthWeb, which had been worth over a billion dollars a few months earlier, for essentially nothing.

My crack editorial and dev team had EarthWeb running with Internet.com within a few days, and the two together were an advertising powerhouse. Between the two sites, we probably had 200 different websites covering all types of Internet and developer tech topics. As for the Hidary brothers, they had had a great ride. But like so many Internet entrepreneurs of the time, they believed their own hype.

BEWARE OF ICARUS

One lesson entrepreneurs must remember is to listen to carefully, and think through, the advice they get from smart people.

Hardly a week goes by that I do not think about a lunch meeting I had in February 2000 at the Harvard Club in New York City with one King Harris. King comes from a wealthy Chicago family, whose assets at the time included among others the Harris Bank of Chicago. King was also an investor outside of the bank. At the time I met him, he was the largest stockholder of the public company Penton Media. Penton Media had acquired my media company, Mecklermedia, in November 1998 for nearly $300 million cash. The Penton team, led by Tom Kemp, were adamant about not owning the Mecklermedia websites, known as Internet.com. The reasoning was that one could not make money with a website, and that Penton's earnings would be hurt if they held onto this part of Mecklermedia. The solution for Kemp was simple: purchase Mecklermedia and then sell 80.1% of the website assets back to me for $18 million. Such a transaction would enable Penton to avoid having Internet.com included in its financial reporting. And if I was successful with making Internet.com profitable, Penton could benefit without a negative hit to its profits.

Another reason for shedding the Internet.com asset was that the Penton management was inept in the Internet space. The whole team had spent their careers immersed in print business-to-business magazines, and so did not believe in the Internet media website model, even though they were purchasing the Internet World trade shows in the U.S. and around the world.

Interestingly, the concept for selling off the website assets to me had originated with the failed deal we had struck with Clive Hollick and United

Business Media of England. Hollick and his management team were even more scared of Internet media than Penton's. They lusted for the trade shows and companion print magazines.

Back to King Harris. Harris wanted to pass on some sage advice to me, specifically that I should consider putting a financial "collar" on my Mecklermedia stockholdings. (A collar enables a large holder to place a Put on shares so that one can lock in a large profit should the stock go into a free fall. Most large Wall Street firms have departments that are willing to take on such risk in the hope that, in fact, a stock will actually increase in price.) At the time of the Harris meeting, Mecklermedia was trading in the high $70 range and my paper valuation was close to $1 billion. I remember sitting at the Harvard Club and thinking, as Harris offered this sage advice, that I was close to being a paper billionaire! I also thought that I should hold off taking his advice until I surpassed one billion dollars—a real Icarus blunder!

Looking back at those heady, go-go Internet days, it was near impossible not to think the future was bright and that one could easily double or triple one's net worth in the coming year. Also, even though I was only vaguely acquainted with Mark Cuban, I should have followed his path when he placed a collar on his Yahoo shares and locked in a billion or more dollars, regardless of what happened with Yahoo's stock price. Only six weeks later, Jack Willoughby's "burn rate" article appeared in Barron's and the Internet stock crash was on. My shares dropped from about $76 a share to a few dollars a share in a period of a few weeks. Oh well. I did not listen to King Harris, and so I am stuck with woulda, coulda, shoulda.

FRUSTRATION WITH CORBIS IMAGES

Five years of my career was deeply tied up with online stock image business. One particular saga was one of my "almost" sales to Corbis Images, which was owned by Bill Gates.

Corbis, as far as I know, never made a dime for Bill Gates. It was essentially his hobby, and probably also a toy in which his losses could offset a tiny part of his income. Corbis had numerous CEOs during my five years in this business (2003-2008). One fellow named Steve was a very nice, sweet fellow who built up the business. But every move ended up in increasing losses. After Steve left, a fellow named Gary took over. Gary was one of the dumber people I have ever come across; if Bill Gates ever had a chance of making money with Corbis, Gary made sure it would never occur. In 2007, after Gary took over, Corbis had not made a strategic move into what was then called microstock ($1 images that came from user-generated content). Microstock revolutionized the stock photo business and made several entrepreneurs hundreds of millions to billions of dollars (see Vignette 17 and my encounter with Shutterstock and iStockPhoto).

By 2008, I realized I had to get out of the stock photo business. I'd borrowed too much money to purchase stock photo companies and there was a bad financial climate, which later became known as the Great Recession. Among my potential buyers were Getty Images, Corbis and a few other smaller international players. Getty was most desirous of our assets, but the deal made the most sense for Corbis because we had a microstock business they lacked, as well as several other low-priced subscription offerings that would round out Corbis' offerings and shortcomings. Gates pretty much allowed whoever was CEO of Corbis to make acquisition decisions, after which he would provide the funds. Frankly, I doubt Gates had a clue about the nuances and directions the stock photo business was heading. Gary chatted with me a few times, and it seemed a deal could be had for a reasonable price. But Gary went off and bought — for much more money — a Canadian outfit that was strong in the traditional royalty-free side of the business that would soon be worthless. Not only did Gary make the wrong purchase, he also made the worst possible acquisition that he could make. It was the equivalent of investing in horses and buggies at the dawn of the automobile industry. Gary did not comprehend the power of the $1 image and the strength of the microstock revolution that was bringing creative destruction to the traditional royalty-free and rights-managed stock photo business.

VA LINUX GO GO

Internet.com had its IPO in June 1999. This was the second IPO for me, following the one for Mecklermedia in February 1994. Internet.com was a conglomeration of perhaps 100 or more websites, covering a range of developer topics and offering originally written news about the business of the Internet and World Wide Web. Our stock offering was priced at $14 a share, but the IPO did not do well for several weeks after its debut. The price declined to about $9 a share before it slowly increased; by October, it had surpassed $30 a share. I remember well that the day I met with Jack Ma for breakfast, in October, I was feeling incredibly wealthy, as the stock had moved into the mid-30s. There was a lot of pressure on CEOs of public Internet companies in those days because mutual fund managers and stockholders, by this time, expected Internet stocks would go straight up. It was not uncommon for stocks to move upwards by double-digit percentages several times a month. Any kind of decent press release could move a stock hugely. In addition, all of the Wall Street banks were running a continuous string of Internet conferences at which public companies would present for 30 minutes to attendees (typically, fund managers and large investors), followed by a 30-minute Q & A, during which the fund managers could ask more detailed questions of the presenter.

I was very good at presenting and even better in the Q & A sessions. After one of these sessions, I would generally see the Internet.com stock jump 20 percent or more within minutes of the meeting's completion. I remember one time, a bank held a conference at a Utah ski resort. As I remember it, Internet.com jumped from the high $30s a share to close to $50 a share within minutes of my finishing my presentation.

It was an unbelieveable, even surreal, time. The crazy part of being involved in all of this was that one started to believe that the hype would last forever.

During the later months of 1999 and into early 2000, the first Linux boom took place. A company called VA Linux went public at $30 a share and closed at close to $300 on its first day of trading, making all the founders paper billionaires! Linux was a natural topic for Internet.com to add as content to its websites, which were already covering Web development and software. After seeing the VA Linux explosive stock valuation, I decided to add a Linux site or two to our collection of assets. After consulting with some of my top writers, we offered to buy some tiny Linux websites that had no revenue and were covering the Linux sector on a very vertical or select basis. Our announcement of our move into Linux, that Internet.com would be covering the field in-depth, caused our stock to jump about 15 percent. There was no revenue gain here, but Wall Street and day traders salivated over the fact that Internet.com was now in the Linux field. I believe I purchased four small Linux sites as the basis of the Linux channel at Internet.com. (When the crash came for Internet stocks in April 2000, Internet.com's stock dropped from about $76 to $6, and VA Linux dropped from several hundred dollars a share to single digits as well.)

My involvement with VA Linux started around 2006, when both Internet.com (now Jupitermedia) and VA Linux (now Sourceforge) almost merged. It was to be a merger of equals, to use Wall Street parlance. I had become business friendly with the CEO of Sourceforge, Ali Jenab. Both of our companies at this time were selling at about $6 a share. However, Sourceforge had $60 million in cash and Jupitermedia had debt of about $80 million, created over its binge of buying stock photo companies. The deal was a natural, and both boards were in agreement about the merits of the deal. Ali had decided to move on, and I would become CEO of the combined entity, which was to be called Jupitermedia. The brilliance of the deal was that the combined companies would now have a great balance sheet because Jupitermedia would be able to pay down much of its debt and still have some cash. Also, because Jupitermedia still had the Internet.com assets, the mix of products would be great and the combination would be a real powerhouse for Web developers and the software community. The plan hopefully would then have Jupitermedia sell off its image libraries. All was grand and agreed to, but, unfortunately, both companies needed the public shares to remain close to $6 a share. That didn't happen.

Jupitermedia's shares floundered as we got close to announcing the deal, which forced Ali and his team to remove themselves from the deal. It was another disappointment for me, as I had come up with a creative structure that would have worked for all parties and stockholders, and which would have bailed me out of a debt overload. As I have written elsewhere, this debt and the great crash of 2008 would create a great crisis for my company and for me personally. Fortunately, my constitution had been toughened and tempered by fire over many years of working in a startup mode, as well as the ups and downs of being an entrepreneur. I chalked up the disappointment of not making the deal to just one more setback of a career that had many, as well as many wins.

Sourceforge ultimately became Geeknet, and got the billionaire Ken Langone to back it and become its chairman. It ultimately sold for about $140 million to GameStop. The other interesting connection to this company is that my angel investor from 1993, Jim Mulholland, Jr., also made an incredible financial killing by being an early investor in VA Linux. Jim had a great eye for early-stage media investing.

INSIDE FACEBOOK

It was a risky deal, but it seemed like a sure winner to me. It was 2010, and anything called social media was a hot media product. I had attempted to purchase Mashable, and have outlined earlier how the deal seemed sure to happen, only to have the owner, Pete Cashmore, pull out as we were about to close. Things had gone well with our acquisition of the AllFacebook blog from Nick O'Neill, but I kept feeling that Inside Facebook, a blog based in San Francisco started by Justin Smith, was the more important property in terms of market share. Justin had put together a great writing team, led by editor-in-chief Eric Eldon, and had a very good business development person in Susan Su. Perhaps the most impressive asset was a product called AppData, which compiled on a daily basis the most-popular apps on Facebook and whose data was being sold on a subscription basis.

Facebook was emerging as a powerhouse; it was about to go public. Apps were launched on Facebook every few seconds, and Facebook could make or break an app merely by allowing the app to be on the Facebook platform.

To me, AppData was the gem of Justin Smith's stable because it was not dependent on advertising revenue. It was a subscription service that was growing rapidly. The subscriptions were sold either monthly or annually, and because the app business was taking off, AppData seemed to be a must purchase, not only for those in the app business, but also for a host of analytical firms and Wall Street banks trying to get a handle on the Facebook ecosystem. This white hot sector had annualized sales jumping at over 100 percent a year, so along with AppData and the blog Inside Facebook, we would be gaining terrific assets for a new and vibrant industry.

Justin knew he had great properties and drove a hard bargain. After several meetings, we settled on a purchase price of $7 million in cash and $7 million in stock of our public company, then called Mediabistro. I was reluctant to use so much cash, as our cash position at the time was about $10 million, but decided to roll the dice, primarily because of AppData. The deal was consummated. AppData continued to thrive, and sales continued to jump. However, within a few months of the purchase, we suddenly faced the departure of Eric Eldon. While I did not realize during negotiations how important Eric was in terms of his staff, I soon understood that Eric's leaving was a bad omen. I had figured that Justin Smith could hold the team together, but soon faced the difficult conclusion that Eric was the key to the whole business. The writing staff idolized Eric, and when he jumped ship to take over editorial control of TechCrunch, several of Inside Facebook's young writers followed him to his new home. And then Susan Su, who was instrumental in running business development, decided to leave as well. Justin was still running overall operations, but things were not the same without Eric. Even Justin seemed lost without Eric and Susan. The AppData product continued to thrive and, fortunately, the team behind collecting and reporting its data was content to hold the course. But within a year, Facebook decided it would no longer supply the information it had been providing free to AppData; the product lost valuable information and lost traction. I knew the importance of the Facebook data, and knew we had no guarantee of permanent cooperation from Facebook, but it was still a tough blow when the spigots were turned off. Justin soon lost interest in the whole endeavor, and so, in less than two years, the acquisition turned out to be a dud.

Part of this decline was caused by the fact that while apps continued to be a vital part of the tech and social media world, the allure of our information was no longer vital for a startup, as there were other ways to launch apps without depending on Facebook. This was also about the time that social game leader Zynga went public, and then went into rapid decline. This somewhat reminded me of the decline in Internet values in mid-2000, which lasted for a few years. It was tough to live through yet another bust, seeing the value of my public company decline rapidly once again. Worse, unlike the recovery of Internet valuations from that downturn, this time the small to middling players in the space never recovered.

Mashable is a great example of the crash in values. At one point, around 2014, it was rumored that Mashable was being acquired by CNN for more than $200 million. While Mashable exits today, it is a mere shadow of what it was, and its value is probably 10 percent of its supposed sales price of years earlier.

In addition to this acquisition turning out badly, perhaps the worst part of the whole experience was the hostility I encountered by the remnants of the editorial staff after Eric Eldon left. One writer in particular was the most entitled person I have encountered in 50 years in business, and incredibly dishonest besides. Overall, it was not one of my better performances as an evaluator of a business or of employees. Justin Smith was a very nice fellow, but in the end it turned out that he had a great idea and had hired terrific people. Those people were the assets that were needed to keep the business thriving. (Facebook changing its data sharing policies did not help.) Inside Facebook was perhaps the worst deal I ever made, and one that is hard to put behind me.

ENTREPRENEURIAL INGREDIENTS/ WORK PHILOSOPHIES

MY BUSINESS PHILOSOPHY
AND FIRST BIG BREAK

I started my first business in 1971 at the age of 26, working out of a small house in Weston, Connecticut. From my study, I launched a quarterly journal that reviewed micropublications (documents and archives published on microfiche and microfilm) for the approximately 3000 research libraries worldwide.

Microform Review was immediately successful, both critically and, to lesser extent, financially. I soon added a database directory of all the micropublications worldwide. This was followed, in 1975, by the launch of a small trade show (my first event foray) for micropublishers and the library community. The show was a success and was written about in *The New Yorker* magazine.

A pattern was established by 1995 that I did not comprehend: I'd find a topic that needed a specialty publication; add a database and some monographs on the topic; and start an event. I have used this formula over and over again. Examples have included CD-ROM, optical disks, virtual reality, HDTV, multimedia, baseball history, antique wooden boats, white-collar crime and, of course, the Internet. At one point, I had 27 journals or newsletters, and several related conferences.

My main problem in these early days was cash flow. I thirsted to find an investor, but had no experience in this arena. Fortunately, my accountant introduced me in 1980 to a Swedish publisher, Rolf Janson. His company, Bra Bocker, based in Helsingborg, had a publishing program and a very successful book club. Wanting to make some small investments in the USA, Janson purchased a 50 percent interest in my Meckler Publishing for $600,000.

I had a fine relationship with my Swedish partner. But they grew tired of my inability to produce profits. Rolf and his lieutenants could not fathom how I could or would continuously create new publications or events. They had a point, as this was my business flaw. Their American lawyer even accused me of being dishonest — a crushing accusation. After 10 years of frustration working with me, and with a push from their attorney, they wanted $1 million for their shares. Fortunately, a German publisher named Klaus Saur of Munich, Germany, had expressed interest in purchasing my various assets covering the micropublishing industry. So I sold these assets to Saur and paid off the Swedes. (Saur was a fascinating character, whose father was Albert Speer's top aide in World War II, and who spent much time with Hitler in the infamous bunker at the war's end.) I simultaneously sold all my media assets that were not technology related. Now I had a company covering CD-ROM, virtual reality and a new, exciting area, the Internet.

Shedding Bra Bocker was a huge win for me, as I regained 100 percent equity in Meckler Publishing. Selling it cost the Swedes at least $140 million, based on what was to happen over the next few years.

GREAT EMPLOYEES

I have been an entrepreneur for more than 50 years. During that time, I guess that more than 2,000 people around the world have worked for me. Most of these employees, and many of the freelancers, were terrific in a variety of ways. A few were stinkers and even crooks. But a very few were so outstanding that to this day I am amazed how great they were, and how they made it possible for me to succeed.

No. 1 in my heart is Tony Abbott. Tony started working for me back in 1975, fresh out of college. A poet at heart, he awoke most mornings at 5 a.m. to write poetry before heading out for the work day.

Besides being a gentleman and an all-around nice fellow, it became apparent early on that there was nothing in the editorial process that Tony could not learn, digest and then excel at. From 1975 to 1995, when he "retired" at age 43 so he could write children's' books, my guess is that Tony oversaw the editorial and production of over 1000 monographs and reference books, countless issues of magazines and journals, immense micropublications of botanical specimens, and the creation of some of the first websites in the world. Tony and I even started an ambitious line of baseball history publications, including the autobiography of one-time Major League Baseball front-office executive Lee McPhail.

On top of all this, Tony was just as well-versed in preparing and editing author contracts and negotiating author royalties. And even more amazing, he never complained when I came up with a new publication or editorial project every few weeks.

We would have lunch several times a week with fellow staffers or our writers, and he was my confidant and sounding board about all things.

Tony and I made the first website purchase in the world. In 1994, we acquired TheList.Com from two feuding partners based in Chicago. TheList was an online directory, by area code, of Internet Service Providers in the U.S. and Canada. It was a brilliant concept that made us a profit of close to $1 million a year for many years (until ISPs were no longer necessary to connect to the Internet). Its model was based on the old Yellow Pages, or what Google does today selling top listing positions to the top bidder. So if there were 40 ISPs in an area code, they would be listed alphabetically (there were about 3000 by 1997). But if one company wanted to be viewed first, it had to pay a significant monthly fee.

Since no website had ever been acquired before, Tony and I could not turn to an attorney; there was literally nobody in the legal field familiar with the Internet or concepts like page views. How did we come up with our offer? We analyzed TheList's profit, of course, but overall we came up with a model for this first acquisition, and many to follow, in which we put a monetary value on page views (at this time, the concept of "unique visitors" was unknown).

Today, Tony is the author of perhaps 70 or more fiction books for children under 12 and is best known for his series "Danger Guys." Tony was and is a one-of-a-kind dream editorial employee.

Another incredible person was Nancy Melin Nelson. Nancy had been a research librarian at several colleges and universities, and then turned to the scholarly publishing world. She edited "Computers In Libraries,"my main magazine at the time, but did much more. She was brilliant at conceiving of the programming for seminar programs at my original events in the library technology space. In 1985, I created a library tech trade show by the same name, and although I sold it in 1995, the show continues with its new owner all these years later. Nancy was the brains and the face of the show. And as new technologies entered the research library world, she would learn about them and immediately find people to be speakers at our annual events in Washington, D.C., Toronto and London, England. When we learned about the Internet in 1990, she immersed herself in the topic and knew every person in the world who could "talk Internet," getting most of them to help us launch seminars. In fact, the first Internet World trade shows, starting in late

1993, were programmed by Nancy. Many of these shows would have three tracks daily and run for two or three days. Like Tony Abbot, Nancy never tired and never failed.

Much of my financial and critical successes are thanks to these two, incredible individuals.

WHY TRADE SHOWS GROW AND DIE

I have started dozens of trade shows, going back to my first one in 1975 called the Library Microform Conference. Held in New York City, it was interesting enough to be written about by the famous *The New Yorker* writer Lillian Ross in her "The Talk of the Town" column on December 22, 1975.

I well remember chatting with Lillian as we walked the small exhibition at the old Biltmore Hotel near Grand Central Station. I was amazed and flattered to have such a famous writer visiting my first-ever conference and exhibit. She was genuinely interested and fascinated that several hundred librarians and publishers from near and far had come to the event. She was well known for books and interviews with Ernest Hemingway, John Huston, J.D. Salinger and many others, and here she was, treating me as though I was the most interesting and fascinating person she had ever met! She started off her piece with the following: "The peppiest bunch of librarians we've ever seen were around the Biltmore the other day in droves attending the First Annual Library Microform Conference, which was pulling them into the computer age." Lillian went on with in-depth reporting about products and conversations with several attendees and a lengthy discussion of my background. All in all, it was a wonderful start to a career producing events by having an interview in *The New Yorker*.

It was financially successful, and I produced several more iterations. But by 1979, it was losing money because paid attendees and exhibitors had declined. Why did this happen?

The lesson learned is that when a technology show is created, it lasts as a successful endeavor only as long as the topic covered continues to evolve, so that attendees will continue paying registration fees to keep abreast of market developments. As soon as evolution stalls, one can count on declines in both attendance and exhibitor booths, followed, inevitably, by the death of that particular show.

I have seen this happen several times during my career. A great example was a show I created in 2001 called WiFi Planet. WiFi technology was not widely understood or used in 2001. I'd read an op-ed article in *The Wall Street Journal* by Andy Kessler about what seemed like a great future technology. Kessler was bullish about WiFi, and so I jumped on the topic.

The first show was scheduled for September 12, 2001. In fact, my team and I were scheduled to fly to San Francisco the morning of 9/11 from New York's JFK at approximately 11 a.m. In the aftermath of the 9/11 terror attacks, the show was suspended, of course. But it launched in Santa Clara in December 2001. IBM was the overall sponsor, and we had about five exhibitors and 100 paid attendees. Within a year, as WiFi started to catch on, the show saw explosive growth. I thought I had captured "lightning in a bottle." By the spring 2003 event, we had more than 15,000 square feet of paid exhibit space and about 600 paid attendees.

But then, the curse of no evolution set in. The next show was a disaster, with 20,000 square feet of exhibit space but only 150 paid attendees. And that was the end of WiFi Planet.

This happened again on a show that I owned called Inside Social Apps. The 2011 event in San Francisco had nearly 1000 paid attendees and 50 exhibitors. But while apps continued as an important part of the smartphone world, the need for a trade show declined as those in the business had learned all they needed to know about apps — and had no need to pay $600 or so to learn about them. The next iteration of Inside Social Apps saw just 10 exhibitors and only 100 paid attendees. Disappointing for sure, but the point was proved.

As I write this book, I have started a new event in the field of quantum computing called Inside Quantum Technology. I have an inkling that quantum computing will be a huge industry, and that I will be in the middle of this growth with a new research endeavor and a website of the same name. Only time will tell if my "inkling" is right.

THE PEMBERTON LESSON

Way back in the 1970s, I had a successful media startup for research libraries. I had spent 18 months learning the scholarly publishing field with two small companies, and when a good idea came to mind, I went out on my own in June 1971.

The business was built around a quarterly journal called Microform Review that reviewed scholarly micropublications (collections of research materials that were published on what was, back then, high tech: microfiche and microfilm).

I charged libraries about $80 a year for four issues, each of which reviewed about 15 collections, such as all the congressional hearings on microfiche ($15,000) or The League of Nations Papers on microfilm ($50,000). Within a year, I had about 2000 libraries as subscribers, and I soon started a small trade show on the topic, as well as a print database of all micropublications, listed by author, title and subject.

It was a sweet business, and was reasonably profitable.

One day, a fellow named Jeff Pemberton came calling. Pemberton had been part of *The New York Times* publishing program and was an expert on the fledgling business of offering data online. He had an idea. Why not copy my model of providing research information for research libraries around the world, but instead of focusing on micropublications, focus on the topic of how online databases could be used by the research library community.

We had a nice chat and compared notes. Then Pemberton suggested that I invest $20,000 or so for 25 percent of his new company. This was the first time anyone had ever suggested to me the concept of an entrepreneurial investment. I was intrigued, but had no idea about what "online" meant. Plus, I doubted that Pemberton would succeed. Jeff was a lovely fellow, but I did not think he necessarily had the "right stuff" as he was considerably older than me.

Pemberton more than succeeded. His quarterly journal, appropriately titled ONLINE, was an immediate hit, and he handedly surpassed my paid circulation at Microform Review. He then started a small, eponymous trade show, but was able to charge much more than I was charging for entrance to the seminars. His topic, I soon learned, was hot. And he attracted many more exhibitors than I was able to get for my Library Microform Conference.

I ran into Pemberton about 18 months after his launch and was envious to learn that he was doing several hundred thousand dollars in revenue, and that he had surpassed my business trajectory by at least 300 percent.

From that day on, I always remembered that I had to focus and be open-minded when new ideas or investment opportunities came my way. To this day, I always listen or read any proposal that comes to me for investment in my VC fund or be considered for a media startup. So the Pemberton Lesson is always on my mind. Be open-minded before outright rejection. One never knows when and where the next great investing idea might come from.

Interestingly, Jeff Pemberton and I were fierce competitors for years in the library reference and technology field. But because I learned from rejecting Jeff back in the mid-1970s, I was always open to experimenting and trying to create new publications for libraries in the tech space. Many were marginal successes or failures, but then it was because of Jeff Pemberton that I jumped into the Internet space — and we know how that turned out to be a huge win.

CFO LETDOWN

I was chairman and CEO of a public companies from 1994 to 2015. A growing and profitable business makes life easy for the CEO and the CFO. It is really important to have a great CFO watching one's back, particularly when there is great growth, but also when things are not going smoothly.

When I first went public in 1994, my accounting firm of Arthur Andersen was concerned about the CFO on staff and had me make a change for the actual public offering. Our growth was incredible, and soon it became apparent that even the new CFO was not up to the task of properly caring for the financials. In fact, I had three different CFOs in a period of 12 months until we righted the ship in the eyes of our outside auditors.

From 1996 on things went great, and the CFO of record did great work. I became dependent on this fellow because numbers were not my strong suit. We sold the public company, Mecklermedia, in October 1998 to Penton Media. The return was about 10x in cash from the February 1994 IPO.

I went public again in June 1999 with Internet.com, with the same CFO in place, and by early 2000 our valuation was well north of $1 billion. The Internet crash in the spring of 2000 destroyed our public valuation; our stock price declined from $76 a share to below $1.

The comeback for our company was selling stock photos online. The change was dramatic. It involved recognizing the industry, and then buying lots of digitized images and companies. This required a CFO with the ability to keep up with rapid movement. Unfortunately, both my previous CFO, who became the COO, and the person he selected to replace him as CFO failed miserably.

First, let me say that the fault was mine. As CEO, I made the mistake of staying with personnel too long. My Achilles' heel in business has been to be too loyal too long and not think of myself. In hindsight, I knew that both of these fellows had to be moved out, but I waited too long. Unreliable numbers killed our chances of success. The signs of trouble had been present for a few years in that I could not obtain good projections. My COO got so "into" his position that he worried more about his power than about stepping in and getting in control of the financials. And thinking back to those days, he should never have become COO. This fellow bungled a great opportunity, but again, it was all my fault for staying with the wrong personnel for too long.

CREATING A SUCCESSFUL B2B TRADE SHOW

My first trade show was in 1975. The Library Microform Conference, held at the old Biltmore Hotel near Grand Central Station in New York City, was forever memorialized in an article by Lillian Ross of *The New Yorker*.

The show was a critical and financial success. It was a small show compared to my later successes, such as Internet World and Search Engine Strategies, but it filled a void for a niche vertical tech topic that seemed to have growth potential.

Regardless of size or profitability, successful business-to-business trade shows all need certain ingredients in order to be considered financially successful. First and foremost, one needs a great event idea. Having first-mover advantage is also important because it is difficult to overcome momentum in a new field. When I started Internet World in San Jose, another established trade show company ran a competitive event on almost the same days in nearby Santa Clara. We knocked them out in every way, but nonetheless it was a nerve-wracking experience. And costly. Years later, I ran a successful 3D printing event in New York City at the Javits Convention Center, and an upstart from England ran a competitive event on the exact same days a few blocks downtown. I had to spend an extra $150,000 on promotion to make sure we were seen as "the" show. It worked, and we were successful (and the other show cratered as a result), but the effort and investment wiped out a good part of our profit.

The next ingredient for success is having a community. Pre-Internet, the community was created around a print journal or a print newsletter. Investment in building circulation was the order of the day. The basic concept remains: your community gets news and other information on a timely basis, and then comes together for the trade show associated with the publication, newsletter or website. Currently, with website publishing and email newsletters, the community is getting information daily, but the idea is to keep the community focused on the trade show or shows. In fact, the website can be a loss leader, produced only to promote the events and other services. Of course, it is all the better if the website and companion email newsletters can attract paid advertising and are profitable.

Having built and sold many such properties, I have learned that large media companies will pay much more for a group of assets that include community and companion products, such as trade shows. I have seen competitors flounder for the lack of a companion trade show.

After a good idea and first-mover advantage, one has to hope that the show's topic is one that will have many good years of evolution and change, so that more and more companies will enter the space to become exhibitors, and more and more paid attendees will sign up for seminars.

When I started Internet World in 1993, there were few commercial offerings in the Internet space. However, there was tremendous interest in learning about the new technology — so while we got only a handful of exhibitors, we attracted about 1200 paid attendees, and that made the show profitable. I would call such an event a seminar until the exhibitor/sponsor revenue is larger than the attendee revenue (even though this type of revenue will be growing too). At that point, it is a true trade show. Once one achieves critical mass (i.e. costs stay flat but revenues explode upwards and margins climb dramatically), one has a very profitable enterprise.

The trade show business is a great business, but everything has to go perfectly. In my case, success predominantly happened because I was first with an event in a new technology field. Going way back, I created the first events for library microfilm (1975); Videodiscs (1979); CD-ROM (1983); library microcomputer technology (1986); HDTV (1988); Internet (1992); Virtual Reality (1992); Search Engines (1999); WiFi (2001); Nanotechnology (2001) and many more; and, most recently, I have launched a Quantum Computing event (2019). Many of these efforts looked good, but by their second or third iterations they were failures, either because the technology itself had "no legs" or the new field was not attractive enough for companies to spend money on exhibiting.

NEGOTIATIONS

The entrepreneur, to be successful, will have to do lots of negotiations. These may involve raising funds to dealing with people, including bankers and VCs, to buying and selling assets. I have done more than 400 deals in my career. Most ranged from $100,000 to several hundred thousand dollars, plus a sprinkling of multimillion-dollar deals.

I became great at sizing up the person on the other side of the table. I dare say that in less than two minutes I can tell if I am deal-smarter or not. I can also tell if the other person is an asshole or a nice guy. Another asset is being able to tell almost immediately if the other side, along with its related advisors, are deal-makers or deal-breakers. (This is particularly true of attorneys.)

I had a deal with one of the biggest jerks I ever dealt with when I sold Mediabistro in 2015. While the fellow on the other side was decent enough, it soon became apparent that he had no social grace and was incredibly rude when it came to responding to phone calls or emails. The deal was completed, but only because I desired to complete it. Thus, much like playing on a team, one has to put personal feelings aside in order to win or be successful.

I also came across several opponents who would get fixated on some aspect of an asset or liability that was trivial to me. These types were willing to torpedo a deal over their fixation. Once I saw this happening, I immediately would go into what I call "option clause," meaning I'd become flexible and offer multiple options just to get the other side to focus on getting the deal done. Several times, I had attorneys or advisors warn me I should not offer this or that option to get a deal done. But these warnings are a deal-breaker mentality, and come from people who have lost sight of the big picture, which is to *get the deal done*. I particularly remember one instance worth retelling on the sale of the asset Internet.com to the public company

Quinstreet. Quinstreet would not complete the deal unless one of my best developers agreed to work for them, which he did not want to do. They also required another developer to be able to fly to the West Coast as needed at their expense. Both conditions were deal breakers. I solved the first by giving a large cash bonus to the first developer. The second issue was solved by creating a complex agreement about how and when this developer would fly to the West Coast if a problem could not be solved online or by phone. This debate, and creating the agreement, was handled by me, as my attorneys could not digest all the nuances and the cost in billings, which would have been sizable. We got it done, but the Quinstreet person who was so consumed with this, never used the agreement or called the developer. I sort of knew this to be what was going to happen, but realized I had to assuage the other side and get the deal done.

This can be particularly tricky when one has a public company. I lost one deal in 2015 because both the outside attorney for my company and a board member were so concerned about being sued that they stymied another bidder from making a much better offer for an asset they were selling. This can be terrifically frustrating.

Overall, I take the responsibility for some bad decisions when my gut thought was "do it" but I stupidly listened to advisors or colleagues who were scared of their respective shadows. The worst case was my board back in 2007. They were so scared of class-action lawsuits that they cost me and our stockholders a $350 million deal. This incident, which involved Getty Images purchasing Jupiterimages, is probably my biggest regret in business (even bigger than not listening to King Harris when he told me to place a collar on my shares in 2000).

Ironically, some of those board members do not speak to me today due to some other matters that cost them some money. They ought to be more upset that because they were so scared back 2007, they lost out on millions in stock options.

AWARENESS

After many years of creating businesses and products, I've come to realize that "awareness" has to be in one's DNA or it is doubtful they can be a successful entrepreneur.

Entrepreneurs have to have the "awareness gene" to everything around them, from reading to entertainment.

Having this skill is actually, for me, tiring. My mind is constantly, without any effort, wondering about many things almost every waking minute. For example, I can walk into a store and immediately wonder about the operation, the inventory, the design and many other things. Just the other day, I walked into a local newspaper store in Manhattan and started studying how many products were crammed into the shelves in this cramped environment. I speculated about what handy items could be added or removed to this small space, where one could find nail clippers to playing cards to whatever. I wondered how the owner had decided what to add or subtract; I wondered if there was a specialist out there who serviced the store and knew that a small newspapers-and-lottery-tickets store needed "this and that" because this consultant or expert had studied what was sold on whims or necessities. This carried on to the small offering of magazines: if the store only had room for 20 magazines, how did the owner decide which magazines to offer? The same awareness plagues me when I'm watching the check-ins for a flight or an event. I immediately start thinking of making the process more efficient, whereas others, I am sure, are just standing there getting bothered about the lengthy check-in. Of course, this applies to airplane boarding too. I imagine how each airline has a team and mock-ups of cabins, and how they must play over and over again the boarding process to try to make a better "mousetrap." I have lots of ideas about this process, although I am not sure any would work.

The point is, my mind is racing on every flight about the boarding process, the TSA security process, or how baggage is handled. All of this is a burden, but it is this mental activity that leads people like me to create business ideas (some good, some bad). Elsewhere in this opus I have written about creating CityBikeBasket, and how I came up with the idea by walking to work in New York City. It is a perfect example of awareness, of what happens to an entrepreneur in daily life, and how ideas pop into an entrepreneur's mind.

This awareness is always present, even when one is reading or watching a movie or play. It also takes the form of imagining — that is, placing oneself in the shoes of a character in a book or movie. A lot of this is being a daydreamer at heart. In my elementary school days, I was often accused of not concentrating or listening to a teacher. Although this was probably my dyslexia at work, my mind was not wasting time. I have mentioned in the introduction to this book my childhood ideas for "Pepsi Pops" and football helmets. Later, as a young father, I remember thinking about how to improve diapers (an idea I did not act on, but which is now part of all diapers).

Over the years, I have had many ideas for movies, including one about the USS Indianapolis tragedy and optioning an obscure book about the tragedy. Unfortunately, my constant awareness and all the ideas that are spawned has led me into trying to take on too many disparate businesses or lines of business, which has sometimes led to financial distress.

I find it hard to walk away from a great idea.

Take my foray into publishing baseball history books in the 1980s, when I should have been concentrating on my technology publishing businesses. Similarly, there was my foray into creating a print newsletter in the 1980s about antique and classic boats, emulating a well-known car magazine called Hemmings Motor News. That idea came about because I had a summer home on Lake George in the Adirondacks. I bought a restored wooden runabout. While chatting with the owner and chief restorer, the idea hit me that the old boat market could use a Hemmings-like publication. The gentleman running the boatyard confirmed to me there was no such publication. And within weeks I started Antique and Classic Boat News, a bi-monthly containing a feature story and a classified section. In retrospect, I see the money I spent money on that launch would have produced better results for my technology publishing products. Antique and Classic Boat News lasted for two-years, but despite a circulation of 10,000, I could not get enough classified ads to keep the newsletter running. I probably lost $25,000 or more, which was painful when my other business at the time was not profitable. Also around this time, I embarked on publishing a series of baseball history books, including a quarterly journal called Baseball History (see Vignette, "Baseball History").

As if an antique boat magazine and a baseball history imprint didn't add enough to my plate, I also started a bi-monthly newsletter called White-Collar Crime Reporter (see Vignette, "Being Curious"). I was at a school function for one of my children and met a fellow parent who was a famous white-collar attorney in Manhattan. A week later, at another school function, I met yet another attorney in the same field. The idea of covering this field seemed like a natural, so I contacted both attorneys, who confirmed such a publication was needed and that it was a great idea. Within a few weeks, after putting together an august editorial board, I announced the publication. I even started a related seminar. White-Collar Crime Reporter was marginally profitable, and I sold it in the 1980s

along with several other titles to Greenwood Press.

Alas, I could go on and on about such endeavors. Most of these ideas were not financially successful. They failed not because there wasn't a need for these niche publications but because I lacked the financial resources to produce multiple publications in diverse fields. And I was unable to entice investors to back my ideas. Nonetheless, like an opioid addict, I could not walk away from a good idea. What was behind this "disease"? Awareness! My life and my awareness DNA produced idea after idea after idea. I still fight this temptation today. However, I now can walk away from these ideas as I am now in my 70s and do not want to get into team-building beyond my interests in 3D printing and quantum computing.

BEING TOO NICE

I have written a few times about my experiences with rescuing Jupiter Research, saving it and selling it. My years were brief with Jupiter Research (2002-2006). It was quite a time, as I bought it when it was running on fumes and sold it when it was pumping out profits and growing robustly. My contribution was recognizing and cutting the bloat, recognizing the underlings who could drive growth (particularly an ex-West Pointer named Kieran Kelly), and spotting that what we now call paid search was going to be white hot and adding it as a research practice. This vignette, however, is about selling Jupiter, nor saving it.

At the time I decided to sell, the one suitor that made the most sense was Forrester Research. Forrester was a competitor and much larger. In 2006, it offered $19 million for the assets. However, I fretted that many at Jupiter would lose their jobs in the aftermath of a consolidation. I felt a loyalty to the feisty Jupiter team and felt they should keep their jobs. So I ultimately sold to a private equity fund for about $13 million, feeling I had done a good deed in saving the jobs of my former employees.

Unfortunately, I was naïve to think that the buyer would not turn around and flip Jupiter to Forrester about a year later, making a tidy profit of several million dollars. When things got bad in late 2008-2009, I could have used those millions. Again, one of my major faults was being naïve about human nature, and I paid a price.

FOCUS

I started my own business in 1971. I had a great idea: review microfilm publications for research libraries. The idea came to me while working for Greenwood Press, a scholarly publisher in Westport, Connecticut. I was a very young director of marketing, tasked with selling multiple thousand dollar historical collections on microfiche and microfilm to research libraries.

I was on a sales trip, stopping at various colleges and universities in New England. During a drive between Durham and Hanover, New Hampshire, the thought occurred to me that there was a need to review these expensive publications for the librarians being asked to lay out thousands of dollars for publications like *The Congressional Hearings* ($15,000, at the time). On my next leg, which took me to Kingston, Rhode Island, I pieced together the business plan. I would call my publication *Microform Review*, publish it quarterly, and sell an annual subscription for $20.

Over the years, I have found that some of my good (and bad) ideas come to me while driving or walking. Motion seems to be an idea generator for me. I have mentioned that I was always a daydreamer in class, and while I was not thinking of business ideas, my mind was always thrusting out on dreams of being a professional baseball player or whatever. As I have also mentioned, awareness is a key to being an entrepreneur. Over and over again I have realized that my thinking and dreaming is special, and that many close friends and even my family do not have this trait. They might be successful, but the success has been linear. Nothing wrong with that, but being able to thrust out in different directions with radical or outlier ideas is rare.

Now, this awareness has gotten me into lots of trouble. From 1971 to the early 1990s, I too often jumped at every new idea that came into my head.

Rash actions, such as starting new publications or events that were not related to some of my more successful ventures, caused me to have cash flow problems and face bankruptcy quite frequently. Looking back, I realize I found it very difficult to pass on an idea that struck my fancy.

Fortunately, in 1990, I ran into a fellow named Alan Klavins, a media banker, former special forces soldier in Vietnam, and the brother of a family friend. Alan was interested in possibly helping me sell my company or selling some of the many publications. During our second or third meeting, Alan turned to me and said I needed focus in a big way. He pointed out that it was great to be publishing 27 journals and newsletters, but that I was covering library science, baseball, white-collar crime, advertising practice, communications law, literary bibliography and more! It was clear that he could never find a buyer because my offerings were too diverse and random.

It was focus or bankruptcy. At about the same time, a friend of mine who was and still is very successful, offered similar advice. Over dinner one night I told him I needed to raise money. He knew of an investor who loved scholarly pursuits, and he thought that this fellow might find it appealing to invest. Within days, I had the meeting.

After about 20 minutes, this rather urbane gentleman said to me something like, "It's impossible to follow the different directions of your publications" and that he thought that I should focus on what might bring the best financial results by shedding many of my offerings.

These meetings, coming one right after the other, were life-changing. Within a few weeks, I started selling off many of my publishing offerings and closing others. I decided that I would hone Meckler Publishing to be a technology publisher for research libraries. Thank goodness I did this. Once focused on technology, my awareness led me to the Internet era, which my daydreaming led me to fantasize about the minute I heard the term "Internet" in March 1990.

HIRING THOUGHTS

Looking back, I have always had a sort of "go-to" person to cover my back and take care of details and administration. Interestingly, in a career of 50-plus years, I have never been able to adapt to having a secretary. Originally, I could not afford a secretary, and I was a very good typist — able to type over 80 words a minute. I also possess a great memory, and can always remember dates, documents and files down to the smallest detail. Besides, I could never understand why people have assistants or secretaries place calls for them. My philosophy was, and continues to be, that if I have to call someone, I do it immediately and I do it myself. On the other hand, there is the matter of delegating and being able to "let go" so that employees can move ahead with clear instructions to take action.

I have witnessed countless entrepreneurs who get blinded by little stuff and cannot relinquish overseeing every phase of a startup or young business. People have always been amazed at my ability to have confidence in the people I have hired, and the way I allow them to take actions to grow operations. Readers of military history might be familiar with Ulysses Grant, who wrote clear and brief dispatches to his generals during the heat of battle. The generals had no doubt that they were empowered to take action, and they knew what they had to do. And Grant replaced those who could not act decisively once his orders had been issued.

Running a fast, growing business is similar to Grant's approach to military orders. However, first and foremost, one must make good hires and evaluate these hires immediately. If they cannot perform within a few days, one must get rid of them and find a replacement. In my own career, I once hired a fellow named John Walsh, who worked for me from about 1973 to 1977. And there was the incredible Tony Abbott, then a 24-year-old. There was simply nothing he could not do or accomplish. Tony was with me from 1977 to 1995. I also had a great CFO, who became my right-hand man for many years. But he got in over his head when I made him president and COO. My greatest mistake in business was not moving him out when it became apparent he had a nasty streak with underlings. He was fine around me, and often invaluable. But his influence became too great and it cost me at least $300 million. After this fellow was terminated, I relied on another wonderful fellow named Mitch Eisenberg.

TURN DOWNS/
RAISING FUNDS

RAISING MONEY, SETTING THE STAGE

For an entrepreneur, cash flow is a critical and often a painful topic. For me, the years between 1979 and the summer of 1993 were full of angst. It wasn't uncommon for me to have 10 credit cards going simultaneously to keep my business operating. Payroll and accounts payable were always on my mind. Even so, I continued coming up with new ideas and rolling out newsletters and journals for the research library community.

The field I had selected was fun and important, but of zero interest to venture capitalists. In my late 40s I was not "bankable." Lacking other financing sources, credit cards were my salvation.

And when I came up with what I thought was a publication that might go beyond the library field, and perhaps attract venture capital, I was stymied by being a few years ahead of my time. Actually, this happened to me several times, notably with my media plays in virtual reality, CD-ROM, and the Internet.

The closest I came to "hitting a winner" was when I became the first publisher to produce information about using CD-ROM, a storage technology that had recently arrived on the scene. In 1986, I published a book by Judith Paris called "The Essential Guide to CD-ROM." The book was immediately successful, selling a few thousand copies in its first few months of publication. One day in the fall of 1986, I got a call from a fellow named Min Yee, who told me he worked directly with Bill Gates of Microsoft. Yee said Gates wanted to work with us on distributing the book, and wanted to have a face-to-face meeting to discuss a venture. He flew from Seattle to Philadelphia, where I was running a trade show on the topic of optical disks. The call alone was astounding. The interest and his "demand" to meet was surreal.

Yee arrived late one afternoon. He was a large and bulky fellow in his late 20s. He was all business as he sat down with me in my hotel suite with an assistant of mine named John Paul Emard. Yee got right to the point. He pulled out a checkbook and wrote a check for $35,000. He said he had a contract with him, which was shocking. He said Gates wanted all the rights. In other words, the book would become a Microsoft book. And I thought I was discussing a joint venture! Yee went on to say that Gates was planning an event in Seattle called "The New Papyrus" that would focus on the future of CD-ROM and digital publishing. He explained that a companion book by the same name of the Microsoft event had been delayed and that Gates wanted our book (in the form of a Microsoft imprint) to hand out at the event. And there was no way Meckler Publishing could appear in any form in the Microsoft edition.

This was a lot of money for me, but I turned down the offer, saying that Meckler Publishing had to receive some type of credit in the front of the book. Yee was dismayed and perturbed. He went back to Seattle, the Microsoft conference was produced, and the original Papyrus book — which I suppose they rushed to complete, having no alternative — became the swag for each attendee. My book was very successful, but of course it would have been nice to have had a Microsoft connection and be associated with Bill Gates. It was not to be. But it would not be my last interaction with Bill Gates.

GO RANCH BET

It was about this time that I earnestly started my own fundraising efforts. Such fundraising efforts remain incredibly vivid in my memory because many caused profound pain and, in some cases, tears.

It is 1991. I have four children, aged 11 to 16. I have large credit card debt. I have decided to bet that my coverage of CD-ROM, virtual reality, and the Internet will make me a fortune. I still own the modestly successful Computers in Libraries magazine and its companion trade show. Although profitable, these media properties cannot support my investment in these new technologies.

Not being able to raise funding, I decided to mortgage my Manhattan co-op apartment, which I owned free and clear. I obtained a $400,000 mortgage, pledging my housing and the well-being of my children. I decided to go all in on personal rick because of my belief that I finally was on the path to profitable business success. Looking back, I was insane to take such a risk with the mortgage. But, then again, entrepreneurs are risk-takers. I was, as they say, "making a ranch bet."

FIRST FUNDRAISING EFFORT

In 1990, a fellow named Tom Cottingham called me out of the blue. Tom had created a print newsletter company called Cobb Group, based in Louisville, Kentucky, which he'd sold in late 1990 to what was, in those days, a giant publishing company, Ziff Davis. Later in that decade Tom founded TechRepublic.

Tom was still overseeing Cobb Group in 1990 and continuing to build his now-sold company. He had come across Meckler Publishing and our fledgling Internet World newsletter, which had started in the fall of 1990. Tom felt I was on a great path with Internet World, and wanted Ziff Davis to consider investing in its future.

Tom pitched me about selling Meckler Publishing to Ziff Davis, or at least doing a joint venture in the Internet media space.. At the time, along with Internet World, I had a virtual reality publication and a CD-ROM publication. He thought that all three topics, but particularly Internet World, had a bright future.

Tom introduced me to then-CEO of Ziff, Philip Korsant. I remember being very nervous prior to the meeting, which happened to be the first day of the first Gulf War, in January 1991. Ziff was the god of tech media publishing, and so I was very confident that my Internet World newsletter, with an investment, could be turned into a magazine. My pitch to Tom, which he endorsed, was for Ziff to buy 50 percent of Meckler for $500,000, and that I would use these funds to invest in growing my titles to a stage where Ziff would take over and turn them into technology magazines.

Korsant was courteous to a fault. He listened to Tom before hearing my pitch. But within 10 minutes, I knew I was wasting my time. Korsant had not a shred of knowledge about any of our coverage areas, and was particularly incredulous about the claims I was making about the future of the Internet. He was a very proper-looking and courteous fellow. Looking back, I realize that while Cottingham thought highly of me, Korsant saw a 47-year-old library publisher who wasn't making a dime. He wasn't the last. Over the next few years, I saw this reasoning in the faces of several potential investors. One person actually told me this to my face!

I kept up with Tom's ventures. For several years, we would meet, email or phone chat. And in 2007, I almost purchased one of Tom's many tech start-ups.

I take my "hat off" to Tom, whom I'll always remember as the first tech media person I came across who "saw" the Internet's potential. Korsant , meanwhile, left Ziff and was replaced as CEO by Eric Hippeau. I did not know it then, but over the next three years I would have several meetings with Eric—and all were classics.

RAISING MONEY DISASTER

The first Gulf War, in January 1991, crushed me and almost forced me into bankruptcy. My big payday, annually, came from my Computers in Libraries conference and exhibition, whose profit of about $200,000 covered my operating expenses for several months. The 1991 show was scheduled for Oakland, California, in early March. That year also was the first time I would try out the idea of an Internet event called Research and Education Networking within the Computers in Libraries conference.

But when the coalition ground assault into Iraq started on February 24, people were afraid to fly because Saddam Hussein had threatened to take down airliners. Yes, our show went on, but it lost money as paid attendance shrank by half. Short of funds for payroll and accounts payable, I made the difficult choice to mortgage my co-op apartment in Manhattan.

Desperate for capital, I decided to advertise in *The Wall Street Journal* for funding. The copy read: "Cutting-edge tech media company offering 50 percent equity for $500,000." The ad, which ran for two weeks, produced what seemed to be one solid lead. A media family from the midwest had recently sold one of the two major daily newspapers in Tulsa to its competitor; they were looking to deploy some of these funds toward media enterprises.

My go-between on the deal was a nice fellow named Ralph. When we chatted on the phone, Ralph seemed very sincere, and upon meeting him in person my reaction was justified. Ralph told me that the family was very interested in my offering. He came to my Westport, Connecticut, office (I was a reverse commuter from Manhattan) for a day of conversation. This led to dinner the next day, and hours more conversation. Ralph reported that his employers were particularly intrigued about the future of the Internet (readers should know that the World Wide Web was not known at this point).

Next in the potential deal with the midwest group, a fellow named Charles came to New York to most likely certify Ralph's positive reports about me and Meckler Publishing. We had dinner at a restaurant on Lexington Avenue near Grand Central Station that Charles claimed was his favorite in New York City. Interestingly, I found it pedestrian at best. He was a nice-looking and super confident fellow, much like Ralph. The meeting went well and so it was agreed that I would fly to the midwest and meet more family members, plus a fellow named Bill (who was the most important family member in terms of making an investment).

Unfortunately, there were no non-stop flights to the city in question from New York. But the lengthy travel sped by because I was positive this trip was going to result in a great funding deal. Ralph met me at the airport and I started the rounds of meeting family members. Before the big dinner, I was introduced to Bill, who was older than the others I had met and was noticeably standoffish. "Explain the Internet," he said. I sensed difficulty with Bill. I explained the Internet protocol and its packet addressing scheme, technology, but he could not fathom how information could be delivered this way. Within a minute or two I knew Bill did not get it, nor did he want to get it. He was one of many people I met over the next 30 months who must have choked years later when they saw my company sell, a few years later, for close to $300 million.

The next day, Ralph joined me for breakfast at my hotel and broke the news that the family had vetoed going forward. Ralph now had a different attitude, probably because he loved my pitch but was now defensive.

On my several-legs flight home, I had to fight back tears. Depression set in. Once again, my naïve nature and belief that everyone would see my visions about the future of the Internet (and how my magazine and soon-to-be trade show) would be immensely valuable had set me up for disappointment.

I never heard from any of these midwesterners again. And I never forgave them for not repaying me for the airfare and hotel.

LONG ISLAND MEDIA GUYS

I cannot remember how I was introduced to Michael Leeds, whose family owned CMP, and Ken Cron, who ran its operations. At the time, CMP was one of the three largest tech media companies in the U.S., along with Ziff Davis and IDG. When I met with them in New York City in early 1993, I made my usual pitch: half of Meckler Publishing for $500,000. This would have given CMP rights to my Internet World newsletter, which I said would soon be a magazine. At the time, neither Leeds nor Cron were believers in the Internet, and Cron, in particular, was a bit incredulous that this 48-year old library publisher might be on to the next big thing in tech magazine publishing.

We had a few meetings. Finally, Cron called me one day to suggest we meet for lunch at the Brasserie restaurant in New York City. Once again, I naively thought I had a good chance for some type of deal, as Leeds, whose family owned CMP, was very enthusiastic.

Much to my chagrin, Cron got to the point rapidly. He pulled out a piece of paper and drew a simple graph. He stated that the Leeds family paid him to build and find properties that had "hockey stick" growth trajectories. He then placed a flat line next to the hockey stick and said something to the effect of "You have a 20-year record of flatline products." I gulped and said the usual "I understand" etc., but at that moment I knew clearly that Cron was clueless about what was going to happen with the Internet.

I packed my briefcase and once more walked away from a meeting in a disappointed state of mind, not to mention having been insulted by Cron's graph. He had a point about my record and he was in a lot of good company with other Internet doubters.

About 18 months later, Leeds and Cron tried to make up for lost time by purchasing NetGuide, a print publication from the media critic Michael Wolff. NetGuide was a compilation of websites, sorted by subject. It was glossy but had no real value because it was not online and was updated manually by Wolff.

According to Wolff in his hilarious book about that time called *Burn Rate*, both Leeds and Cron, upon closing the deal, jumped up and down and shouted, "We bought the Internet." In fact, they had been taken to the cleaners by Wolff. They later started a magazine by the same name, although it was never more than a lame competitor to my Internet World magazine, as Netguide floundered rapidly. For several years they tried in vain to create an important print publication covering the Internet. They even attempted to compete with my Internet World trade show. But everything they did failed. Their saving grace was having United Business Media to pay $1 billion for CMP in 1999— an overpayment of at least $500 million.

Cron and Leeds were just two more of the many who missed buying into the ideas of a 48-year old library publisher who just happened to have caught lightning in a bottle.

SMUGNESS DOES NOT PAY

In 1992, I came across Allen Brigish, a charming South African and the publisher of several media industry newsletters somewhat akin to a few of the library research titles that I had been developing for many years. Brigish's company had been acquired by Hershel Sarbin of Cowles Business Media. Sarbin had once been a top lieutenant of William Ziff, creator of the Ziff-Davis computer magazine empire.

Tasked with building up Cowles Business Media, Sarbin was acquiring publications and business trade shows at a rapid pace. Brigish, who knew of my work developing Internet World as a newsletter and possibly as a magazine, suggested that I meet Sarbin, as he felt that Sarbin might want to acquire my business.

Sarbin was a confident and fellow and my senior. After several meetings, I once again naively felt I had found an investor or even an acquirer.

In hindsight, it is now clear to me that Sarbin was playing me somewhat, taking a chance that this "Internet thing" might really be the next big technology in business and consumer publishing. After several more meetings at Cowles' and at my office, Sarbin assigned his chief analyst for prospective business deals to continue the discussions.

The analyst was thorough, and spent hours chatting and digging into my records. She also went into the field and asked many other analysts about the Internet.

The bad day came suddenly. Sarbin called me up to say that after spending a lot of time and analysis, that he, with the help of Judy's research, did not see the Internet as being the next great revolution. He wished me good luck, so once again a turndown from an established media pro.

Ironically, the very night of the Sarbin turndown, my wife and I happened to run into Sarbin at a New York City restaurant. We waved at each other.

HAMILTONS OF DENVER

A deal broker named Tom Nugent approached me in 1991 to tell me that he had met the son of an oilman from Denver who had just settled in New York City after living in London and who wanted to invest and work in tech media. I do not remember how Tom Nugent found me, but it might have had to do with an ad I ran in *The Wall Street Journal* trying to raise funding. Regardless, Nugent was a sincere fellow, so I decided to meet with Tom Hamilton, the son of oil magnate Fred Hamilton. Hamilton was as sincere as Nugent. I told him about my Internet plans and other tech media properties that I was developing, and that I hoped to raise at least $500,000 for a reasonable percentage of my company. Tom told me his father had just sold most of his oil and gas operations to a large Australian company, and that the father would consider backing the younger Hamilton by investing in a company such as mine. A meeting was set a few days later at the venerable River Club in New York City. Fred arrived on schedule. I was taken aback by his height (many inches taller than Tom) and his incredible head of grey hair. He looked the part of a western oilman, and he had the airs of a billionaire that he was. I conveyed to Fred my background and thoughts about the Internet. Having recited this many times, I had become astute at reading body language and eye movements. None of Fred's poses were positive. Nonetheless, Fred knew Tom really wanted to be part of Meckler Publishing, and we seemed to hammer out a rough understanding. Fred told me that when he got back to Denver he would have his legal team draft an agreement in which the Hamilton family would make an investment and that Tom would come aboard in some to-be-agreed-upon position.

A few days later, I got a letter that offered the funds, but the conditions were difficult to accept. One in particular made me think that life would not be comfortable with Fred Hamilton looking over my shoulder. It dealt with my car. At the time, I had a several-year-old Lincoln Town Car that I commuted in from New York City for the round tip to my office in Westport, Connecticut. I think the car was in the third year of a four-year lease and had about 70,000 miles of wear. One of Fred's many restrictive conditions was that I could not keep the car; if I did, I would have to reimburse the company for its annual costs. When I brought this up to Fred's legal associate, I was told that this and several other restrictive clauses, which amounted to perhaps $10,000 a year, were iron-clad, and that any request to change them would be a deal-breaker.

As much as the money was needed — and as much as I desired to make the deal — my gut told me that Fred was going to be difficult to deal with and that I would be less than happy having him and Tom as partners. I broke the news to Tom Hamilton, who was crestfallen, but I had the feeling that he, too, knew Fred was going to be difficult to digest. A few years later, I came across Tom Hamilton, who said he had followed the meteoric success of Mecklermedia. He had the look of someone with deep regrets. As for Tom Nugent, I had a few potential dealings with him over the years, and he was always the sincere gentleman I met back in 1991. As for Fred, he was an incredibly generous philanthropist over the years, and was the driving force in building a significant art museum in Denver.

Ironically, I ended up joining the same River Club where I had met Fred in 2010. I saw Fred at a club function and went up to him to remind him of our meeting 20 years earlier. He was still tall and distinguished, but the passing years had turned him into a frail and kindly older man. I realized it was best to just say I had the pleasure of meeting him many years earlier.

INNOVATIONS

SPOTTING THE INTERNET

I was a research library publisher who had veered into being a publisher of technology information and directories for research libraries. By the mid-1980s, my business success required finding new frontiers. My marketplace, 3,000 research libraries worldwide, needed a constant flow of aids for running tech in a library environment.

During this period, I began producing small trade shows, which was to become a throughline in my long and varied career. Trade shows are interesting (and can be extremely profitable) because once critical mass or break-even is achieved, then generally every dollar of increase drops to the bottom line.

In 1986, I launched Computers In Libraries. Computers In Libraries, or CIL, was started after I had purchased a print newsletter called Small Computers In Libraries from the graduate library school of the University of Arizona. The Arizona team, headed by Dean Ellen Altman and a faculty member named Allan Pratt, had created a bi-monthly newsletter in 1983 to help librarians manage the microcomputer revolution spawned by Apple and IBM. I recognized that the newsletter could be the basis for a magazine and an event, and become the "go to" source for library microcomputer information. As I have done many times, I followed the path of creating a community around a publication and then starting a conference or trade show related to the publication. This move was really the forerunner to my ultimate success with Internet World.

The CIL conference, which at its height featured 20 seminars and 50 exhibits, took place annually in Washington, DC, London, England, and Toronto, Canada. Initially, I moved the U.S. venue around the country, but eventually settled on Washington, D.C.— mainly because of the Library of

Congress. It was not uncommon for the Library of Congress to send 30 to 50 staff to our event.

The conference was a three-day affair. And every night, along with my editors, I would take at least five librarians out to dinner. The conversations nearly always revolved around new tech trends and what might be needed in the way of a new directory, newsletter or guide.

At the March 1990 conference, a librarian named Marietta Plank from the University of Maryland was one of these dinner guests. My custom was to ask each guest the same question: "What is the next big thing in library technology?" That night, Marietta's answer became my Holy Grail.

"The Internet," she said. Marietta was sitting to my immediate right, and I distinctly remember saying to her, "What is the Internet?" She reminded me, as did Eric Flower, a librarian at Georgia Tech and editor of CIL magazine, that Eric had recently written an editorial in CIL extolling the future of what he called "The Super Electronic Highway." All the guests, including Tony Abbott and another employee, Nancy Nelson, became eager participants in conversation about what the Internet was and what it might become. I was keeping notes for good ideas and wrote down the following: "Start newsletter for the Internet."

I naively thought "this Internet thing," which seemed complicated to use, would only be used in research libraries. But I instinctively saw it as a great next step in the delivery of information.

Since starting my publishing business, I had seen the switch from microfilm/microfiche to optical disk/CD-ROM. The Internet, I immediately grasped, could change research options and deliver information on almost any topic, nearly instantaneously.

My next steps were onerous. I had always found it easy to find a librarian who, for a fee, would be willing to take on a freelance job to help produce a bimonthly newsletter. But there were few if any experts in the nascent Internet field. In fact, there were few librarians who knew what the Internet was. Honestly, it was frustrating. The few who entertained the job told me they doubted that there were enough developments in the "Internet field" to support more than a few pages a year. Bimonthly reporting was out of the question!

Finally, I found a librarian at the University of California, San Diego, who said she would tackle the project, but with a caveat: the newsletter would be quarterly, not bimonthly, and no more than four pages.

The first issue of Research and Education Networking was published in October 1990. Why that title? Because nobody knew what the Internet was back then. The first issue launched at a major technology-in-education trade show in Atlanta. The main sponsor was Apple.

I brought 300 copies to give away at my exhibit booth. I doubt 20 were taken. It was a depressing disaster. Over two days, I had a few conversations with semi-interested attendees. But my disappointment was unavoidable. I had gone to Atlanta thinking I would garner at least 50 or more subscribers.

Regardless, I am fairly certain that Research and Education Networking was the first commercial publishing effort in the Internet space.

Looking back, I could have given up. But I was undaunted and dogged. I started promoting the newsletter with a subscription price of about $70 a year for four issues. (This might seem expensive, but library periodicals are very expensive.) The first year brought in only about 50 subscribers. Success would have to wait for another 18 months and a name change to Internet World.

BEGINNINGS OF INTERNET WORLD TRADE SHOW

I started the Internet World newsletter in the fall of 1990. Originally called Research & Education Networking, the newsletter became Internet World in early 1993.

I used the unwieldy name Research & Education Networking for a trade show started as an add-on to my Computers In Libraries event in Oakland, California, in the spring of 1991, then morphed into Electronic Networking and Publishing in January 1992, and finally became Internet and Document Delivery World in December 1993. The December show took place in the keynote hall of the Javits Convention Center in New York City.

About 1100 people registered for the conference program at Javits. I was ecstatic! The exhibition also attracted about 20 organizations, but only two or three were actually what could be classified as pure Internet "plays." Two of the exhibitors were early Internet Service Providers (ISPs), including PSINet and Netcom.

O'Reilly Associates, a well-known technical book publisher, introduced its Network Navigator online Internet service at the show. O'Reilly's exhibit drew the most interest. A few months later, O'Reilly sold the service to America Online for about $20 million. While a nice payday, I have speculated that the sale precluded the O'Reilly owners from becoming billionaires, as they were, at the time, light years ahead of everyone in providing connection to the Internet.

Network Navigator was the beginning of countless deals in the Internet space. During the early years of the Internet World trade show, there were many start-ups that were snapped up by larger organizations, such as Vermeer

Technologies, which was purchased by Microsoft at Internet World Boston in 1995.

No convention center or hotel had Internet connectivity in the early-to-mid 1990s. I had promised attendees that they would be able to see the "Internet in action." So, months before the event, I interviewed a variety of so-called experts who promised me they could bring Internet connectivity into the Javits Center. The small company I engaged for this task kept assuring me right up until the exhibition hall opened that all was well, and that we'd have connectivity. Finally, the fellow came to me as the show opened and said that he needed 1000 feet of special cable to complete the job and fulfill his promise. He also told me that the electricians union at the Javits Center was impossible to work with, and that they were hindering his ability to bring connectivity to the show floor.

Because he was working feverishly, he asked if I could go and get the cable from an electrical supply store two blocks from the convention center. So there I was in my business suit, walking to the store, getting the several hundred feet of cable, flinging it around both shoulders and hiking back to Javits. Unfortunately, it was a futile exercise, as my expert failed. On the other hand, most of the show-goers were not disappointed. Never having had Internet connectivity, they were fine with videos and other visuals in the meeting rooms and on the show floor.

These were the days of long-forgotten programs with names like "Archie," "Veronica" and others that fired up the imaginations of entrepreneurs and start-ups. I would not be surprised to find out that it was at this show that a young Jeff Bezos first cut his eye-teeth on Internet knowledge.

The show was a huge success for Mecklermedia. We made close to $400,000 on the event, mainly due to the 1100 paid attendees who jammed the meeting rooms to the rafters and crowded the few exhibitor booths. The feeling throughout the hallways was electric.

Mecklermedia had just published a print directory called On Internet, a print directory of every Internet resource in the world. We brought 400 copies of this $35 directory to the show and sold them all. Little did I know at the time that this print guide was actually more comprehensive then what Jerry Yang and David Filo were dreaming up at Stanford, which would soon be introduced as Yahoo! But I was essentially a reference book publisher who did not quite comprehend that I was fueling a revolution. Looking back, On Internet, which we should have put online in December 1994, could well have been a colossus in its own right.

During the first day of the show at the Javits, John Markoff wrote a seminal article in *The New York Times* about the launch of something called the World Wide Web. I remember asking my then Internet guru, Chris Locke, what the Markoff article meant to the future of our show and magazine. His response was simple: "The Internet now is multimedia." Again, I did not comprehend what this meant, but knew it was going to make my show that much bigger and better. Of course, I had no idea that the Web was the missing link to unleash the Internet Revolution and Internet Capitalism.

BEFORE ZUCKERBERG

I first heard about virtual reality in 1992 from a freelance writer named Sandra Helsel we were using. Immediately recognizing the tantalizing possibilities, I started a print newsletter and a seminar. From these beginnings I was soon producing a conference.

The first Virtual Reality: Theory, Practice & Promise was held in San Francisco in 1991. Jaron Lanier, the computer scientist, writer and artist, was keynote speaker. Our chairperson, Sandra Helsel, put together a two-day program with a variety of speakers. Sessions included "Virtual Reality and Cyberspace: A Demonstration of the Differences," "Bringing Affordable Virtual Reality Systems to Market," and "Educational Implications for Virtual Reality."

There were no commercial ventures in the field, but Lanier was already a star, and had been doing research into VR for a few years. Because of Lanier (who showed up an hour late for his keynote), we got decent press about the show.

As a follow-up, we ran the event in New York City in 1993. Our PR agency was able to get me on the "Today" show prior to the opening at the New York Hilton, where I remember seeing a mob of people visiting the exhibits.

As with some of my other events, Virtual Reality World was a grind to run. We got publicity galore, but not much revenue. Nevertheless, I was a plunger and I went on to run an annual event in London, San Jose, and New York.

Initially, I thought VR was going to be bigger than my other startup in the Internet space. But by early 1994, it was apparent to me that there was no money to be made in VR and we dropped the show.

(Update: As I write this in 2018, virtual reality has been "resurrected," thanks to Mark Zuckerberg's interest in the area and his purchase of Oculus VR, the developer of a VR headset. While I still doubt VR will be a money-maker, it was nice to be the first event in this space.)

Looking back over 25 years, VR was just another technology in which I "saw the light" years before the technology was ready for prime time. I got lots of publicity (there are several videos on YouTube from 1992-1994 about me and VR), but it was yet another venture where I made no money. Fortunately, the Internet tsunami was building. It was the one time that being first paid off big time!

IMPACT OF
INTERNET WORLD
TRADE SHOW

In his recent new book *How the Internet Happened: From Netscape to the iPhone*, Brian McCullough argues that the Internet craze can be traced to the Netscape IPO of 2005. He is wrong.

For those who were present and deeply involved in the beginnings of the commercial Internet, I think there can be no doubt that the launch of Mecklermedia's Internet World trade shows was where awareness exploded and where, no doubt, fledgling entrepreneurs like Mark Cuban, Jeff Bezos and others cut their eye teeth. (I recently had lunch with Mark Cuban, during which he reminisced on how Internet World 1994 in San Jose got him pumped up about the Internet.)

It might seem self-serving for me to write about the impact and importance of Internet World, since it was my creation. But I know for a fact that Netscape's big-impact launch was at Internet World in December 1994 at the Washington Hilton in Washington, D.C. Netscape paid my company thousands of dollars to have huge barrels of disks containing its Netscape Navigator Web browser to be given away the entrance to the exhibit hall for three days. (In those days, Macs and Pcs could not readily connect to the fledgling Internet via Internet Service Providers (ISPs) so that users could sign up for the service.)

And it was at this show that we first ran continuous classes on how to connect to the Internet. There was an insatiable demand from thousands of attendees wanting to learn about this way of getting information online.

At the time, Internet World was produced in San Jose in the spring of 1994 and on the east coast in the fall (it went to Boston in 1995 and then settled at the Javits Convention Center in New York City). By the end of 1995, we started producing the event in Malaysia, England, Germany, Argentina, Mexico and Brazil. We had demand from governments throughout the world to bring the show to their countries. I remember the consul general of Hungary in New York City asking me to lunch to prod Mecklermedia to bring the show to Budapest!

Total attendance of our Internet World shows grew rapidly: New York City, 1993 (1,500); San Jose, spring 1994 (3,000); Washington, D.C., fall 1994 (6,000); San Jose, spring 1995 (10,000); and Boston, fall 1995 (25,000). We hit 75,000 at shows in Los Angeles and New York City in 1996, and added an annual summer event in Chicago, where the keynote speaker was Eric Schmidt. By the end of 1996, the event was being produced in 15 countries and growing.

By the end of 1995, our eponymous magazine was approaching 400,000 paid subscribers.

Netscape was significant, for sure, but it was just one of many IPOs in 1995, including America Online's IPO. Also, 1995 was the year that Microsoft finally entered the Internet space and announced its Explorer browser.

HOW DID SO MANY
MISS THE INTERNET?

A 2018 book by Glenn Rifkin titled *Future Forward: Leadership Lessons from Patrick McGovern, the Visionary Who Circled the Globe and Built a Technology Media Empire* is a wonderful tribute to Pat. I have mentioned my dealing with Pat and his numerous attempts to purchase Internet World in the mid-1990s.

Pat, through his IDG umbrella, sued my company several times, claiming that IDG was entitled to any brand that used the word "World." We started using the Internet World brand in 1992, and IDG did not commence legal action against us for several years. He even went so far as to try to own the name "Intranet World." (An earlier vignette discusses the suits; as late as 2016, there was wrangling over my ownership of the URL iWorld.com.)

For all the glorious, visionary wins that Pat had, he missed the Internet. I started in the space in October 1990, and launched a trade show in 1993, as well as a newsstand magazine. All the while, Pat and IDG did not make a whimper of a protest. But starting in 1995, when Internet World came to Boston and sold out the world trade center and attracted 30,000 attendees, IDG began the legal rumbling.

Regardless of the legal wrangling, a quick perusal of the index of the Rifkin book has no mention of "Internet." Kind of shocking. But the reason is that Pat, his colleagues and all of IDG missed the Internet revolution. In fact, IDG never had a serious publication or trade show in the space. Instead, there was teeth gnashing and lawsuits against Mecklermedia. Even to this day, IDG has a legal action against my use of a URL I have owned for many years: www.iworld.com. This domain was originally purchased in 1994 and originally owned by Mecklermedia. I still use it as a website to maintain my rights, and to keep IDG at bay about its ownership claims.

So even though Pat is no longer with us, one of his weird legacies goes back to his missing the Internet revolution and a 20-year legal vendetta.

HAVING A GOOD EYE
BEYOND TECH AND MEDIA

I am convinced that most successful entrepreneurs have a good eye for more than business. To be good at this, one has to be aware. Awareness comes into play in daily life. For example, walking down the street ,or inside an airport, or stroll strolling in a mall, or reading news (in print or online).

Take my interest in military history. In the early 1980s, I read about the sinking of the USS Indianapolis in the Pacific Ocean toward the end of World War II. This led me to a book by Richard Newcomb, published by the University of Indiana Press in 1959. The book was long out of print, and few people were interested in the story, other than it being mentioned in the movie "JAWS" — in the memorable monologue by Sam Quint (written and played by actor Robert Shaw) about hundreds of sailors being killed by sharks in the Pacific waters after the Indianapolis' sinking.

My imagination took over, and I figured the Indianapolis tragedy would make a great movie. I contacted the Indiana University Press and optioned the movie rights for one year or so. Being a dreamer, I figured I would write a screenplay and make lots of money with this great story. The reality was, I hardly had time to run my struggling publishing business and help raise our four children. So the screenplay and the option were put out to pasture.

Fast forward 20-years-plus and there have been several documentaries, TV movies and motion pictures made about the Indianapolis. And even today I have several ideas for movies based on the historical events that I collect. So the dreaming goes on!

In the world of contemporary art, I have had a good eye too. When I was able to spend money, I purchased several David Hockney, Sean Scully and Wayne Thiebaud works. All have had meteoric valuation increases over the past 20 years.

I relate a lot my success, once again, to awareness, historical training and, perhaps, a dyslexic brain. Every day is tiring for me as I dream up business, art and even movie ideas.

A HUGE GAMBLE

Months of research readied me to try ComputerDigitalExpo, which launched in November 2003 at the Mandalay Bay Convention Center in Las Vegas.

I faced a $700,000 loss if this show wasn't successful, but the upside was immense. I rented the Mandalay Bay space in Las Vegas and brought in some ex-Comdex sales people, who started contacting hundreds of Comdex exhibitors, including the likes of Microsoft and Bill Gates' handlers to try to get them to break away from Comdex. Six of my team spent a day at Microsoft with decision makers. We left Microsoft thinking that we had won them over. Our argument was simple and correct: Comdex had lost its way and was not focused enough on the coming digital revolution and the merging of computer, mobile phones and other digital devices. Plus, our show would be more business-focused than Comdex.

The story worked well enough that we signed up about 30,000 square feet of exhibit space. We hurt Comdex, and sales of their space probably declined 40 percent or more from the previous year's event. Unfortunately, Microsoft remained with Comdex and this killed us, even though we had a large presence from IBM and several other notable technology companies. The end result was that I drove Comdex out of business and it never recovered. In June 2004, Comdex cancelled the annual Las Vegas show. If I had kept my CDExpo going, we probably could have tripled space and been profitable the next year, and then been on the road to great profitability. But about this time, I had stumbled onto the online stock photo business; I saw that it would be best for Jupitermedia and stockholders if I placed my efforts in this direction.

JUPITER RESEARCH

My business model is simple. Find a topic and attempt to become the "source" for business-to-business information about it, and then create as many revenue streams as possible. When I went into business in 1971, my model was the R.R. Bowker Company, based in New York City. Bowker had the leading magazines for the library community, had the leading database of publications for all libraries, and had leading print review resources. However, it lacked both an event business and a research business. So when it was my turn to enter the library publishing market, adding these missing pieces was my innovation, and was certainly one of the keys to my future success.

I dare say that the more streams of revenue my model possesses, the more valuable it becomes to potential acquirers. The problem with developing many streams of revenue is that it requires financial resources to keep fledgling operations alive while waiting for good cash flow and, ultimately, profitability. Even today, as I write this book, I am attempting to develop the model for the fields of 3D printing and quantum computing. Both of these new ventures have associated event and research arms. Back in 1993, after I had successfully launched a magazine, trade show and website to cover the commercial Internet, I realized that a startup called Jupiter Research, which offered research and consulting for Internet startups, would be a natural and additional "stream" of revenue for Mecklermedia. As more readers subscribed to our publications and websites, we could help grow Jupiter Research without having to spend heavily on promotion because our own media assets would carry the bulk of its advertising.

Jupiter Research's founders, Gene DeRose and Kurt Abrahamson, had started their company on a shoestring in 1990 and were very interested in selling to us. The problem in making the deal was the dreaded bogeyman of the effect Jupiter would have on the earnings of Mecklermedia, a public company. Jupiter was losing money but growing rapidly. Ultimately, I backed away from the deal, feeling that Wall Street would go negative on the Mecklermedia stock if we bought a losing operation. Only three years later, Jupiter went public and soon had a paper value of $1 billion.

But like so many other early Internet companies with sky-high paper valuations, by the time of the Internet crash in the spring of 2000, Jupiter's stock was almost valueless. By 2002, the company was on the verge of bankruptcy. And that's when I stepped back in. See, I had been watching Jupiter and lusting for it ever since 1995. This time, my negotiations were with an outside consultant, since Gene had left the company when things went south and Kurt was not to be part of the negotiations. By the time I got back involved in the spring of 2002, I was told that the company would have to cease operations within two weeks unless a lifeline was created. The need was one month's worth of payroll and rent. Even so, Jupiter had to vacate its space at Astor Place and find new office space in New York City in less than a month. This necessitated moving about 75 employees and all of the complications involved with an acquisition.

I solved the payroll and cash needs with a one-page document as I sat with the Jupiter consultant brought in to negotiate the deal. I also wrote a personal check for $200,000 to cover payroll. By the next day, I found office space that we took over from an Internet startup called Snowball that had gone bankrupt, but not before the company had done a several hundred thousand makeover of 15,000 feet of office space on Park Avenue South. We got the deal done in less than two weeks and moved the Jupiter team into the new office. Fortunately, I had an incredible "can do" tech team and some solid administrative personnel. Within a month, we refocused Jupiter from about 20 different research services to 12, and started a new service concentrating on the new field of paid search marketing. Paid search was just then developing, thanks to the success of a company called Overture and the birth of Google. This turned out to be a blockbuster research offering that grew rapidly and, in many ways, saved Jupiter. I also made a junior sales person by the name of Kieran Kelly head of sales when the sales director suddenly quit as a vote of no confidence in new management. Kelly was astounding! He made it all happen. We also made bets on junior research analysts to take senior positions, and this paid off as well. By 2005, as I moved more and more into the stock photo business, I decided to sell off Jupiter Research. We sold the operation for about $12 million—not bad for an initial $200,000 investment!

FIRST CEO TO TWEET

I believe I was the first CEO of a public company in the United States to blog, and also the first to actively use Twitter.

My blog (no longer published) was created in 2003 to help launch Computer Digital Expo, my Las Vegas trade show (see Vignette 39). It was an outgrowth of musings I produced irregularly for several years on a website I had owned called Internet.com. I imagine these pieces still can be found online, even if the links are long forgotten. Most of the pieces were about lessons learned in overseeing a business-to-business website in the technology space. However, one I specifically remember was a poignant piece I wrote two days after 9/11, when I got down to the "pit," where the twin towers once stood, and wrote about the devastation.

In those days, I still dressed for work in a suit, tie and dress shoes. As I walked along Fulton Street looking into the pit, I was covered in ash from the fires. And I remember how long it took me to clean off my shoes. I was shocked by how much ash could be seen on the floors, counters and shelves of the closed stores on Fulton Street. I have read a lot about soldier experiences in combat, and a common thread is the smell of death and destruction. I can sense that odor all these years later.

When I started using Twitter in 2009, there wasn't another CEO of a public company tweeting about daily business doings and, occasionally, specifics about financial information. Ultimately, I was contacted by the Securities and Exchange Commission (SEC) and told they were opening an investigation into my use of Twitter. There was concern, they said, that I was providing inside information to Twitter followers to the disadvantage of other investors.

Documents sent by the SEC investigator included a series of questions asking for my rationale for tweeting, as well as my justification. With the help of our outside attorneys, we sent back a comprehensive response of a dozen pages or more. One original defense was that my tweets were being read by *more* people than a normal financial press release, and so I was actually getting the word out much better than the "normal" methods. We also explained that while I tweeted about forthcoming earnings and acquisitions, no investor was at an advantage, since there was no bar to anyone from following me on Twitter. We had many other defenses as well.

In the end, the SEC semi-endorsed what I was doing with Twitter, and if one searches "Alan Meckler and SEC regulation FD," one will see information about how I impacted SEC regulations. In fact, a noted scholarly law journal wrote a seminal paper citing this SEC ruling, endoring the idea that my Twitter use had blazed a new trail in financial public relations.

In just the last two year, when Elon Musk, CEO of Tesla, was accused by the SEC of using Twitter to pump for Tesla's common stock, *The New York Times* reporter Andrew Ross Sorkin wrote that I was the original CEO "public company tweeter."

Musk was ultimately fined by the SEC and his board was reprimanded. Of course, my use of Twitter compared to Musk's is not in the same league. But, I did set a precedent for CEOs using Twitter.

BASEBALL HISTORY

I have always been an avid baseball fan. Love of baseball enabled me to teach myself to read at 7. In the early 1950s, not knowing I was severely dyslexic, I was about to repeat the second grade because I could not read. But a thirst for baseball doings got me to learn to read on my own, through the daily baseball reporting in the many daily New York newspapers that my father brought home every night. There were eight dailies in those days, and as I remember it, we had the *Herald Tribune* delivered every morning to our suburban home on Long Island. In addition, my father would bring home the *World Telegram, Journal American, Daily News* and others. I would pour over the sport sections and, of course, my interest moved to football and basketball when baseball was not in season. It was also baseball that trained my mind to do simple arithmetic for batting averages. To this day, I am a whiz at doing numbers in my head, although I was never able to pass algebra or chemistry, or any course that required formulas or word problems.

During my childhood, baseball games on television did not show stats in the then simple black and white format. Therefore, I computed in my head every average of the Yankees, the Giants and the Dodgers as their players came to bat. Later, when I became a book publisher, the thought occurred to me that there was a dearth of serious baseball history books. I have mentioned elsewhere that these whims and ideas led me to start new lines of business that hurt me financially, because I lacked the cash flow to support a wide range of topics. I had no focus, and found it impossible to resist launching a new product line that I saw as valid and necessary for the marketplace.

I certainly was correct about the lack of good baseball history books. One of my first ideas was to start a scholarly journal called *Baseball History*.

I enlisted Professor Peter Levine of Michigan State University to serve as editor in chief. Peter did a marvelous job, and the journal was well received by the critics. The problem was, we could not get much advertising from book publishers because there were not many companies publishing baseball history. And we could not charge very much for the journal, so we could not cover costs. Nevertheless, our promotions were fun. We gave away commemorative World Series balls from 1987 to any person who subscribed, shipping the ball with a plastic holder. The promotion worked great, and we were swamped, but the revenue received did not cover our operating costs. An interesting aside is that we needed someone to help us pack the balls in special boxes and create labels to send the commemorative baseballs. We advertised in the local Westport, Connecticut newspaper and the packer we selected was a fellow named Jeremy Schaap, then a 14-year-old going to the local junior high school. Jeremy is well known today as a journalist on ESPN and the author of many sports books.

My baseball books were solid. Take John Holway's *Blackball Stars* about the early history of the black leagues. The book received critical acclaim but was not profitable. However, publishing quality books such as this brought in many manuscripts from writers thirsting to get their baseball books published. One day, I got a call from Marty Appel, then of WPIX in New York City and a part-time PR consultant for the New York Yankees. He was helping Lee MacPhail write his memoir and needed a publisher. Lee, who was from a baseball business family, was president of the Yankees and had been with several other teams as an executive. Marty arranged a meeting, a contract was agreed to, and in 1992 we published Lee's autobiography. Reviews were solid, but there still were not any profits for my baseball book operations.

Perhaps the most interesting story from my baseball book publishing career was trying to raise the funds to publish what would have become the definitive book of baseball uniform history (for all major league teams). I had read about Marc Okkonen, who had a hobby of researching every uniform iteration for every baseball team. I met with Marc in the late 1980s with my Editor in Chief Tony Abbott (today, a well-known children's book author). Marc was an interesting fellow, but in order to publish the book, at least $50,000 was needed, due to the book's thousands of color illustrations. I tried to raise the funds from a Swedish publishing company called Bra Bocker, but the book had no appeal for Sweden or anywhere else in the world. Ultimately, Marc was published. He passed away in 2019, and mostly through his book of uniforms he garnered a very large obituary in *The New York Times*. The uniforms book was another occasion where my gut was correct, but a lack of operating capital prevented me from publishing.

I had a few other baseball-related forays, including publishing a bi-monthly print newsletter called *Sabremetrics Review*. Sabremetrics is today the basis of what every major league franchise uses to analyze the statistics behind the movement and signing of baseball players. It is also behind the success of the Oakland Athletics and their general manager Billy Beane, the lead in Michael Lewis' book and, later, the movie *Moneyball*. I learned about Sabremetrics through my baseball book publishing efforts. In 1991, I attended one of the first conferences about Sabremetrics in Albany, New York. I remember being amazed by the seriousness of the sessions and of the attendees. For two days there were numerous seminars. As an aside, the local minor league team called the Albany Yankees was having a public relations lunch at the same Albany hotel as the conference. I decided to observe, and was incredibly impressed by the master of ceremonies, who was one of the most impressive speakers I had come across. His name was Buck Showalter, the manager of the team. I knew right then and there that Buck was a winner and would someday be a successful major league manager. I was right. Buck later managed the Yankees, Diamondbacks and Orioles, and was indeed respected as a great handler of players, public relations and strategy.

I had two more thrusts into baseball. The first was publishing a wonderful paperback called *A Century of Children's Baseball Stories*. This lovely book got great reviews. If I had stayed in the book publishing business, I think this could have been a successful series for both the marketplace and me, finally making some money. Alas, the Internet came along and that was the end of my days as a book publisher. In the end, I published more than 800 books with the help of Tony Abbott, but the baseball books were my real love (and the biggest money loser).

The final baseball angle I played was starting a conference called Baseball and American Society. I produced it with the help and partnership of the library of the Baseball Hall of Fame in Cooperstown, New York. We ran the event for two days, and used the Otasaga Hotel in Cooperstown. Our first keynoter was none other than the well-known Stephen Jay Gould, who unfortunately died a young man. Gould was a Harvard professor and paleontologist who wrote many popular best sellers about science and society. Gould was also a polymath. I remember well his keynote, which was about the extinction of the .400 hitter in baseball. As I recollect, Gould said the main reasons were: relief pitcher specialists, larger gloves, more travel, more games and much more.

The conference received rave reviews from *USA TODAY*. But this was now nearing the end of my book publishing career, as Internet World was starting to grow rapidly, finally giving me a path to financial success. The conference was run for a few more years by the Hall of Fame but without my participation. It was a money loser, but I did snag a lifetime membership card to the Hall of Fame — a nice keepsake.

I remember the whole baseball publishing experience fondly. Our books made a difference, and are valuable to the study of baseball history. But I lost a ton of money. It was just another critical success without financial reward. Baseball book publishing was just one more example of how I had a good idea, but entering this arena took me away from focusing on my best asset: technology publishing.

REAL ESTATE EYE

In addition to spotting tech trends and having a decent eye in selecting contemporary art, I have had good success with real estate. My real estate efforts are related to purchasing property and homes where I have chosen to live, rather than attempting to invest. My greatest success has been on the east end of Long Island, New York.

I remember watching a television interview in the 1980s the with Jann Wenner, creator of *Rolling Stone* and other publications, sitting on his patio in the Hamptons, overlooking the Atlantic Ocean. That image stayed with me for years, and when I started to "hit it big" with my Internet media companies, I began shopping the Hamptons for an oceanfront property. The quest started in August 1993, when I was invited to the Southampton home of Jim Mulholland Jr., who had just made an angel investment in Mecklermedia. Mulholland had given me $1.2 million for a bit less than one-third of my company.

Riding down Meadow Lane in Southampton on a beautiful August morning literally blew my mind. It was a drug-like hit to my mind: the incredible light, the dune grusses gently swaying, the smell of the Atlantic Ocean, and Jim's house sitting by a dune. It was overwhelming. I turned to my wife and said, "Someday we are going to live on this road overlooking the ocean."

In reality, I had less than $10,000 cash to my name, but I was always a dreamer. Later that day, we rented a small, oceanfront cottage in Montauk. In those days, Montauk was a bit seedy, quite unlike the glamor it now possesses. For a few days during our vacation in Montauk, I engaged a realtor to show me properties. I figured that a Montauk ocean property would cost a small fraction of ocean properties further west, and I was correct. Periodically, in late 1993 and early 1994 (after Mecklermedia's IPO), I visited Montauk.

On one of these visits, I bid on a small ocean house. The realtor could not see how I was going to pay the $1.4 million price, but I assured him that Mecklermedia was going to be successful. The owner was in his late 70s and had been trying to sell the house for two years. We worked out a deal with a few hundred thousand down that gave me three-years to pay the remainder. . The owner wanted the house for the summer of 1995, which meant I did not have to make the down payment until the fall of 1995. I was still a free agent, and could keep looking at other properties. In the meantime, Mecklermedia stock exploded, moving from its initial offering price of $6 (in February 1994) to $15 by the late summer. Also, several Wall Streeters approached me about doing a secondary offering, slated for 1995. By the time the road show for the secondary was completed, Mecklermedia was selling at $35 a share, and we split the stock, two for one. Now I had some real money for the first time in my 25-year working life. I told the homeowner in Montauk that I was going to look further east. (He would have had a deal had he not wanted to use his house for the summer of 1995.)

The summer of 1995 was a bit of a buyer's market in the Hamptons. I found a piece of property on the same Meadow Lane as Jim Mulholland Jr. It had been on the market for over two years, and had a building plan approved for a house with a pool. The price: $1.6 million. Several people told me I was crazy to pay that much, but I felt that Meadow Lane ocean property in Southampton was a form of gold. So I took the plunge.

My wife and I engaged American architect Francis Fleetwood (he designed over 200 shingle-style homes in the Hamptons, including ours) to design the house, and 12 months later we were living my dream: a house in the Hamptons, directly on the Atlantic Ocean!

A few years later, with the help of a broker by the name of Tim Davis, we bought a larger piece of land on Meadow Lane and built a larger house. This second house was the home featured in the Nancy Myers movie *Something's Gotta Give* (2003), starring Jack Nicholson, Keanu Reeves and Diane Keaton.

Designed again by Francis Fleetwood, the house and kitchen inspired lots of press and a large following on social media. I now have moved on to another part of the Hamptons, this time to a refurbished ocean house.

The first ocean house on Meadow Lane sold for many times my cost; the second sold for one of the top prices ever in the Hamptons. Along with these successes, I bought and sold an apartment in New York City with a significant gain.

With real estate, as with tech publishing and start ups, I have learned that I must go with my gut instincts. When others tell me I am crazy if I feel good about a deal, I move ahead. In fact, I have gotten into trouble and left a lot of money on the table by being influenced by naysayers, such as the time I did not buy iStockPhoto in 2005 or did not sell Internet.com in 2006, when I foolishly listened to one of my key employees. These were billion dollar mistakes that I think about quite often. However, I have had my share of wins too, and the real estate wins were quite satisfying. Besides, I got to live my dream of having a home on the Atlantic Ocean in the Hamptons. It is not often that one gets to live a dream.

FACING 2008

My first 22 business years, from 1971 through 1993, were fraught with cash flow problems. From the time of my first IPO in 1994, I doubted I would ever have cash flow problems again. Few if any people foresaw the 2008 Great Recession. This crisis caused great damage to the economy, companies and many individuals. I did not escape this tsunami, and it required all of my experience and inner strength, gained from my earlier business years, to come through this turbulent time.

A perfect storm of borrowing funds for my public company, making personal guarantees, and an economy in crisis, almost brought me down. The period prior to 2008 had seen me moving into the stock photo business with Jupitermedia and its division, Jupiterimages. We had been on a torrid acquisition binge, starting with Photo.com in 2003. We purchased about 20 companies or collections in the next four years, for a total of about $125 million. Most of this had been financed by Chase Bank. Chase wasn't our only source of capital, however. During this period, we sold the Search Engine Strategies trade shows and the ClickZ website to Incisive Media for $45 million; we also sold Jupiter Research for $14 million. Chase was so pleased with our growth and progress that they kept assuring us that we'd have access to as much money as we needed.

When a bank throws money at you like this it becomes a drug. It caused us (and me) to become somewhat reckless with business decisions because, the thinking was, "Things will only get better, and there will always be more money from Chase." However, by 2007, Chase started to demand higher interest rates for our loans. So we turned to Royal Bank of Scotland and KeyBank.

The folks at Royal Bank of Scotland were almost drunk with wanting to loan us money. I remember one meeting with bank loan officers in which they were nearly forcing us to take more money. Ultimately, in the summer of 2007, we met with KeyBank, who took over our loan obligations. They too were at the ready to offer funds as we needed them, but these loans were loaded with the usual caveats.

By the fall of 2007, I sensed that the stock photo business was not going well for us and it was time to shed the operations. Corbis Images made yet another offer for our image business, but we turned it down. This was a huge mistake. The offer of about $7.00 a share had a lot to do with our declining the offer. This was the pressure of having a public company weighing on my shoulders and of not wanting to admit to shareholders and fund investors that we had not done as well as we should have done. As we entered 2008, Jupitermedia had debt of about $88 million. Finally, I decided we had to get out of the stock photo business, and we engaged Merrill Lynch to try to sell the operations. The obvious purchasers were Bill Gates' Corbis and Getty Images, headed by Jonathan Klein. There were several other smaller players, but in reality only Corbis and Getty had the wherewithal to make a sizable offer. It was a no-brainer for Corbis to make the purchase, but Corbis had always been losing money, and its new CEO, Gary Shenk, was replacing Steve Davis.

We met with Gary, but it was obvious he was lightweight and did not fully comprehend what Jupiterimages would be able to do for Corbis. Also, I believe that there was animosity left over from our declining, several times, to sell to Corbis between 2005 and 2007.

Looking back, not selling the image assets to Corbis in 2005, for over $550 million, was the dumbest move I ever made, but I had a board and COO at the time who could only see the problems caused by an asset sale as opposed to a stock sale. And being a public company, the optics would not be good because there would have been a large tax bill with an asset sale. Nonetheless, we could have shielded about $125 million of the sale and, after taxes, we would have been a public company with several hundred million of cash and one of the larger tech websites, Internet.com.

Jonathan Klein, head of Getty Images, had always thirsted for Jupiterimages because we were a thorn in his side with our large image library of images, animations, music and clip art. When we first started to compete with Getty with the Photos.com purchase in 2003, Klein scoffed to Wall Street that our images were "crap." Although he was correct, he missed the point that low-cost subscription images were the wave of the future. Within two years, Getty laid out $50 million for iStockPhoto, an operation from Calgary, Canada, that was selling images for less than $1. iStockPhoto revolutionized the royalty-free, stock photo business by offering a marketplace for amateurs with iPhones. Images that were selected by iStockPhoto were offered for as low at $0.99 per photo, and soon thousands of images were flowing into iStock daily and several other competitors in what became known as microstock.

As an aside, my other dumb mistake was not buying iStock for $5 million cash when it was offered to me in 2005 by the founders. At the time, it had just finished the year with $300,000 in sales, but once again I did not go with my gut instincts, and the rest is history. Today, iStock is worth well over $1 billion. The other mistake here was that the founder of Photos.com had created a test product line called Rebel Artist in 2002, which offered the same service as iStockPhoto. When we acquired Photos.com, I made the decision to have the founders concentrate on Photos.com and not to spend time on Rebel Artist. A huge mistake by me. In fairness, my logic was simple: Photos.com was growing by about 70 percent a year, so why would we spend time on Rebel Artist? Imagine if Rebel Artist had been given breathing room! It would probably have started growing at several thousand percent a year! My gut instinct failed me here. Regardless. Klein still wanted Jupiterimages and its huge image library. In late summer 2008, he offered $150 million cash. The cash was coming from Hellman Friedman, a private equity firm in San Francisco that had recently taken Getty Images private, and which included Mark Getty and Jonathan Klein as partners.

Our contract with Klein was nearly completed when the Lehman investment bank declared bankruptcy. I got a call from a senior partner at Hellman Friedman named Andy Ballard to tell me that they still wanted to complete the deal, but because of loan covenants for the Getty deal, which now had problems due to wildly swinging interest rates from the Lehman crash, that they had to drop their offer to $88 million. "This is our final offer," Ballard told me. Wow. What a punch to the stomach. The $150 million deal would have been mostly tax free, and would have set up Jupitermedia nicely to grow its remaining businesses after the $85 million loan had been repaid. Now, although we would still be able to repay the loan, we would have no working capital. It was crunch time.

I decided to play Klein somewhat, and it worked. I knew that Corbis would offer no more than $70 million for the Jupiterimages' assets, but I also knew Klein wanted them. So I told him that Corbis was offering $90 million. Klein did not want Corbis to have these assets, so he caved quickly and offered $98 million, which we accepted. We had to get antitrust approval for the deal. In ordinary times, this might have been difficult, but in the scary times of 2008 we were granted approval rapidly, as the government realized that hundreds of people would be out of work if approval was not granted. Once the deal was completed, we were able to pay off our loan. Plus, this left us with some modest working capital. Jupitermedia was saved.

There are several asides to the story. Merrill Lynch wanted their full commission, based on a $150 million deal. We had to play hardball on this, and ultimately got them to shave the commission by 30 percent. Remember, these were trying times and very scary. If another Wall Street house had collapsed or the financial crisis deepened, Jupitermedia would have had to declare bankruptcy.

The lesson learned from all of this is one I tell all entrepreneurs: money raised or what you have in the bank has to be cherished and relished. That money might be the most important product a startup has. I have seen countless examples of entrepreneurs who were able to raise funds at will, only to see this ability dry up overnight. This happened a lot in the go-go Internet IPO days, and it has happened recently in the cryptocurrency/blockchain arena, and it has happened yet again during the COVID-19 pandemic. It is a recurring problem, but startups and entrepreneurs fail to grasp or believe how critical it is to watch your bank account. I, too, got burned badly by the easy money of 2003-2007.

REAL REAL AND I-ELLA

Timing and luck are everything for the entrepreneur. Be a first mover, and with good luck, one has a shot at success. Recently, The Real Real went public. This slick company resells couture clothing and accessories and, to date, has been a great success.

I saw this market developing many years before RealReal went public or was even created. I came across Ella Gorgla in 2010, the year she launched I-Ella.com. In hindsight, Ella had the wrong brand name, but she certainly had a great business idea— the exact same idea as RealReal. At the time, I was CEO of Mediabistro.com, a website for media professionals that was, among other things, producing monthly "elevator pitch" videos of up-and-coming startups. Ella was featured in one of these videos, and you can still find it on YouTube. Ella had a great education, and had been at IBM in various capacities when she launched I-Ella. She had been featured on the *Today Show* and had won several awards. We did her interview in one take at the Mediabistro offices, and because I felt her idea was a great one, I asked to invest. I personally placed $100,000 with I-Ella after visiting her office near Canal Street in Manhattan.

Ella assured me that all was good, and for a while all seemed good. But, alas, things did not work out, and I-Ella folded two years later. I have not spoken to Ella since the failure, but see she has a significant job in fashion these days. It was painful to lose the investment, but good to know I was correct about the sector, as demonstrated by the RealReal IPO. I look back on this failure and realize again that my enthusiasm and gut reaction about the idea/business was right on. Unfortunately, good gut reactions and business do not always work out for the best. Over the years, I have had my share of failures over good gut reactions and ideas.

BOTANICAL PUBLISHING

Over 50 years, I have made forays into many publishing and media sectors. The lesson in all this is that, for too many years, I lacked focus. I could not turn down a good idea, whether it came from my own head or somebody else's.

Thus, from the 1970s until I "hit" the Internet jackpot, I spent many financial and mental resources going in too many directions. While most of the ideas were solid, they could never be entirely successful because I lacked financial resources.

My imagination led to publishing ventures in white-collar crime, communications law, bibliography, antique boats, baseball and more. Perhaps the most far-out move was when I embarked on becoming the foremost publisher of botanical specimens in the world! I cannot remember what started me on this effort, but I do remember visiting the New York Botanical Garden in the early 1980s and meeting with its head botanist about publishing on microfiche the "type" specimen collections from the garden. A type specimen is the original plant discovered in the field, which is then dried and mounted on large sheets of paper, called folios. Generally, there is only one type specimen in the world. And on each sheet are notes from the botanist, which are likewise unique. A researcher desiring to see the original would have had to travel to wherever the specimen was housed. Needless to say, this could involve thousands of miles of travel and thousands of dollars of expense.

Having had lots of experience with microfilm and microfiche publishing, I was well suited to tackle this project — one that had never been pursued prior to my efforts. And effort it was. A special camera had to be used to film each specimen, and the work had to be done at the New York Botanical

Garden as it was not safe to move some types of specimens from a collection due to their fragile nature.

Our liaison at the Botanical Gardenwas one Pat Holmgren, and she was eager and positive to participate, because she too realized we were making history. Overseeing the project, once the filming was completed, was my ace editor-in-chief Tony Abbott. As I have said, in 20 years working with me, Tony was able to accomplish any editorial task thrown at him. And boy did I throw "tasks" at him. Filming and proofing the specimens was time consuming, but mechanical. The real complexity was creating the printed index that would come along with the purchase of the collection on microfiche (a microfiche measures 4x6-inches, contains 96 images, and is read on a machine designed for the format).

The printed index was a nightmare to produce, but Pat and Tony created a marvelous directory. It can still be found in about 100 libraries worldwide. We sold the collection for $5000; the index could only be purchased for several hundred dollars. The breakeven on the production was about 15 sets, and fortunately we sold many more. This success prompted me to embark on publishing on microfiche many other collections of specimens, including one from the Smithsonian and one from San Francisco's botanical gardens. We also published the United States Department of Agriculture's watercolor drawings of every type of apple in the United States [there are around 800] that had been commissioned as a WPA project during the Great Depression.

Like many of my projects, I became a minor celebrity within the fraternity of experts and aficionados of the respective topics. I was widely known in botanical circles, and attended association meetings where I attempted to find other large collections to publish and, of course, sell. This was not unlike my efforts in baseball publishing, white-collar crime publishing, antique boats and history. Each one of these efforts had critical success, but the drain on my financial resources was staggering. The wider I went, the more I suffered financially and emotionally. But I did love having the critical success that went along with these difficulties.

The botanical collections were ultimately sold to a business friend based in Cambridge, England, by the name of Charles Chadwyck-Healey. It was another bail-out for me at the end of the 1980s, when I was in need of cash to keep Meckler Publishing afloat. We made some money on these collections, but not enough to justify the effort. Again, if I had started concentrating on tech publishing in the 1980s, instead of going in several vertical directions, there is a chance I would have become financially solvent earlier than 1994. However, I always felt that the next foray into a new field was going to be the holy grail for me.

EMPLOYEE HORROR STORIES

An entrepreneur is not going to do well in the short or long term without good personnel. Larger firms use HR departments to interview and vet potential employees. Startups, by comparison, have to use the instinct of the founder. In fact, it is good to be sort of a gun-slinger when it comes to these decisions, by which I mean gut reactions are everything. I dare say I was immediately good at making quick decisions about potential hires.

I remember one time in the early 2000s, my company was hiring a new head of HR. The retiring head helped bring in four final candidates. I interviewed each with my COO, CFO and house counsel, as well as the outgoing HR head. After meeting the four, my colleagues all selected the same woman. I was in favor of another female candidate. However, since my interaction with the head of HR would be infrequent, I agreed to go with the consensus selection. Wow, what a mistake. The woman turned out to be power-hungry, and during her visits to our offices around the country, she threw her weight around and demanded subservience. She caused great problems in headquarters. If this weren't bad enough, within a few weeks she started having an affair with a married employee. While carrying on the affair, she and her employee boyfriend "conveniently" arranged business trips that allowed them to link up for a few days in Florida. The damage caused by this HR honcho was shocking. After six months, she was terminated.

The point in the story is that my gut instinct was that this hire was not wise; I instinctively felt she was a phony. Maybe my greatest weakness is that I like to defer administrative details to others. Yes, this can sometimes be a strength, and not waste time on frivolous matters.

Another mantra I have had is, No Nepotism. Unfortunately, one of my key executives over many years caused me to override this rule. The executive had a bit of a Svengali effect on me, and I allowed him to convince me to hire his brother-in-law. The hire was a nice fellow, and technologically proficient, so he was a good fit for a company that constantly needed computers, WiFi and other tech issues quickly addressed and fixed. But this fellow was a cancer whose shenanigans were hidden from me by the executive brother-in-law.

The tech work required this fellow to go to many of our trade shows around the United States and the world, along with several other male and female employees who were part of the show team. During these trips, this fellow became involved with several unmarried women, and in one case he had a ménage à trois, which my executive knew about but about which I knew nothing. The drama didn't end there. Apparently, the brother-in-laws had a serious argument in the office parking lot with exec's sister, who had found out about the affair. On top of everything else, one of the female members of the sex party, after being terminated, sued my company for millions. It was all very ugly. The outcome was a big insurance settlement for the terminated woman and, of course, the tech brother-in-law was fired.

I should have fired the exec as well, but as I've stated several times, the biggest mistake I made in my career was keeping this fellow around for a few too many years. I have a dear friend who was once head of one of the largest banks in the world. He told me in late 1999, when I mentioned the personality problem of this exec, that I should go to him and say, "You have to change your ways, and if you don't, one of us has to go, and it's not going to be me." I tried this out, and the exec definitely changed (around me). Still, stories popped up every few months about how nasty this guy could be. But for some reason, I could not pull the trigger until 2008 — at least 5 years too late, and hundreds of millions or a billion lost because of the sway this fellow had over me.

So as much as my instincts and gut reactions were great, my one mistake was a catastrophe that haunts me to this day. Over the years, I suffered several double-crosses by employees who ran off with ideas and or who turned out to be disloyal. Overwhelmingly, I was surrounded by terrific people with great stamina and hearts of gold. Unfortunately, the bad cases are the ones that "rise to the top" in telling a business history. Elsewhere in this book, I have written about some incredible gems of people, some of whom continue to work with me to this day.

ONE MAGAZINE OUT OF MANY

The entrepreneur has to be resourceful. Along with being resourceful, one has to adapt, as well as be aware once a new enterprise starts to percolate. A good example during the rapid success of Mecklermedia in the mid-1990s was our fast-growing magazine business. We had started with a print newsletter called *Research and Education Networking*, in the fall of 1990. A chance meeting with Lotus founder Mitch Kapor in 1992 got me to change the name to *Internet World*. By the summer of 1993, the newsletter became a bimonthly magazine, sold on newsstands. The magazine experienced explosive growth, and so we increased the frequency to monthly. But I soon realized there were important "vertical" topics that needed magazine coverage that were not practicable for *Internet World*. So a new bimonthly was created called *Web Developer*. This title, too, was somewhat successful. And shortly thereafter I created a weekly, controlled circulation newspaper called *WebWeek*, which was followed by another bimonthly magazine called *Internet Shopper*.

Mecklermedia at this time was a public company, and while it was extremely profitable, we faced the dilemma of having both growth and profitability while, at the same time, investing in new products. The Internet World trade shows were immensely profitable, growing from show to show. But the magazine business was a challenge, particularly when several competitive magazines were launched by large media companies such as Ziff Davis, IDG and CMP. The solution was to adapt and be resourceful.

By late 1996, I felt that print was ultimately going to be doomed by Web publishing, and that magazines and newspapers would be greatly impacted by all types of websites. I hit on the idea of consolidating our various print properties into one title. I would keep the fabulous brand name

Internet World, but this would now become a weekly, controlled circulation newspaper and I would cease publication of the three remaining titles: *Internet World, Web Developer* and *Internet Shopper.* This meant we would have to terminate several redundant personnel, as we would now have only one staff for *Internet World* the publication and another for iWorld.com (soon to become Internet.com), our website. I selected Rob Hertzberg, who had been editor in chief of *WebWeek,* to become the editor in chief of *Internet World,* and allowed him to select his team from among all of the publications.

The idea was brilliant. We now could concentrate on one print publication, along with building our website. These two assets, along with providing great content, were essentially loss-leaders designed to promote the growth driver of the company: the Internet World trade shows.

Looking back, I believe this move was the culmination of my having learned the lesson of focus that I had lacked for close to 20 years prior to my success with Internet World. Having several magazines was fun, but not practical, particularly as I steered the company into having a business-to-business focus, instead of a consumer focus. Such focus was also a necessity because our competitors were attempting to lure our large exhibitors away from Internet World by saying that our properties were not truly B2B. This was hogwash, but the likes of ZiffDavis, IDG and CMP were desperate to stop the Mecklermedia juggernaut. After all, the leaders of these companies could not believe that a 50ish former library technology publisher with a $2-million-a-year business a few years earlier was crushing them in the B2B space. In addition, each of these companies and their CEOs had turned down my offer of 50 percent of Mecklermedia for $500,000 during the period between 1991 and 1993. And now Mecklermedia had a market capitalization of over $200 million, and was growing rapidly around the world.

MULTITASKING

I am amazed how difficult many people find it to multitask. In fact, I would go so far to say that if one cannot multitask, don't attempt to be an entrepreneur (or, at least, a startup-type entrepreneur).

My initial startup required me to be editor in chief, marketer, bookkeeper and more. Sometimes having so many tasks seems overwhelming. I learned early on to tackle the first task and not think about others until the first one was completed. Maybe being severely dyslexic was an advantage for me (although I did not realize I was dyslexic until I was 57). Looking back, I realize I worked out in my head everything I had to do. No charts, no lists. I have always been able to keep everything straight in my head, due to an incredible memory, which is a characteristic of successful dyslexics. I am not suggesting that the key to multitasking is to be dyslexic. Rather, I am saying that this condition helped me to multitask. A trick I use is to visualize the completed project, whether it be a report, a presentation, or a task. By visualizing, one sees *how* the project can be accomplished. It also helps to be able to adapt to changing conditions or demands. This is a vital skill for the entrepreneur. For example, if one is trying to get an investor or bank loan, the person on the other side of the table is likely to make demands or set hurdles before loaning you the money. It is also highly likely that during the process the lender or investor will change the process or the reporting requested. This is where adapting comes into play. And while this is happening, the entrepreneur might have to tackle marketing, personnel, or personal demands at the same time. It is so easy to get overwhelmed. One has to keep one's eye on the target and the task at hand, and be ready to have several of these tasks going at the same time. The trick is making sure to finish each before starting another task.

My trade show and seminar businesses are perfect examples of the multitasker at work. When I did not have many staffers, I had to run registration, worry about food service, make sure the audio-visual was running smoothly, not to mention check that the seminar speakers were arriving and on schedule. Yes, I always had some help, but I had to keep all of these tasks balanced and going on most of the day. In time, my event businesses grew and I was able to hire excellent personnel to handle some of these tasks. However, there were always snafus that could arise from minute to minute, and I had to be the person to jump in and make the split-second decision to stop a bad situation from getting worse.

The final part of business multitasking in a startup is leadership. Leadership requires a firm self-assurance without being nasty to employees. Fortunately, I was able to win over my employees because they saw I was first to carry equipment, help with registrations, or even move directional signage when needed. Multitasking, adapting, and leadership are musts for the startup entrepreneur.

BASEBALL CARD DEALER DIRECTORY

I am proud of my foray into baseball book and journal publishing, but I would have been better off preserving cash and focusing on technology publishing. I did not see this at launch. As with many of my ideas and publishing thrusts, I always thought that the next thing I started was going to be hugely successful and help me make a fortune. The entrepreneur in me blinded me from being practical.

I remember publishing John Holway's important book *Blackball Stars*, which received extremely positive reviews. I was convinced it would be optioned for a movie, and even played out the plot in my head. Never happened. Movies were always in my mind, however. I have mentioned how I bought the rights to *Abandon Ship* from Indiana University Press about the USS Indianapolis sinking at the end of World War II, and felt for sure I could write a screenplay and get it produced. It did not happen, but at least I had the satisfaction, years later, of seeing countless documentaries, TV movies, and motion pictures made about the tragedy.

This brings me to my last baseball story. In 1987, as I started publishing baseball books, the thought occurred to me that the fragmented baseball card collecting industry might be yet another place where I could create a huge win. My son, then 7 years old, was an avid card collector; we visited local baseball card stores and went to baseball card shows in and around New York City. These trips caused me to realize that there was no overall directory of baseball card dealers. For example, if one traveled to Cleveland or anywhere in the country, a directory would make it easy to find local baseball card dealers. This was way before Google and online search, so the idea seemed plausible. I also figured I could sell advertising in an annual directory, and so I was soon publishing the Baseball Card Dealer Directory. I also decided I could start an annual national baseball card show. Unfortunately, about the time my event was being planned, I found out that a group of baseball card dealers were planning their own event. I attempted to convince the dealers group to throw in with me, since none of them had experience planning and producing events. Their first event took place in Atlantic City, New Jersey, and to this day the national event runs every summer in a different American city.

Undeterred, I went full speed ahead with my dealer directory. To make the directory extra special, I came up with the idea of having an honorary editor. The honorary editor was to be a baseball Hall of Fame member. I paid a nominal fee to these editors, and got them to sign 100 copies. The idea was that these 100 copies would sell for a premium, becoming a valuable collectible. I published three editions of the directory. My first honorary editor was Early Wynn, the famous pitcher for the Cleveland Indians and other teams. Later, Bob Feller was the honorary editor, who was followed by Johnny Vander Meer, who once threw two consecutive no-hitters for the Cincinnati Reds.

The project took a lot of resources and never made money. It turned out that baseball card dealers loved the idea, but they did not have the resources to advertise. Also, many dealers were part-time and did not have stores. Finally, many went into and out of business rapidly. It was a fun project, but a bust.

Looking back, the lesson is that I used my "model" of building a community and then trying to sell other services (an event) to that community. I have followed this model religiously since the 1970s. I honed it, as it produced some modest successes in the areas of library technology, CD-ROMs and optical disks, but it failed with many other categories, including antique boats, baseball cards, white-collar crime, communications law, government documents, small press, virtual reality, HDTV and others. Somehow, I soldiered on, always thinking that the next idea was going to be the big winner. And then, of course, I hit it very big with the Internet.

PARANOIA WINS THE DAY

Capitalism is sport. One can come up with a great idea, and even have first-mover advantage, and a competitor can arise quickly and perhaps overtake you. Andy Grove, a founder of Intel, wrote an article for *Fortune* in the 1990s about his business philosophies. After reading it, the one thought I came away with was that being paranoid was essential for success. I hate to write this, but it is difficult to be trusting in business and life if competition is involved — particularly when it comes to money.

When I started my Internet World venture in late 1990, I realized I had to raise funds. I was turned down by dozens of investors, Vcs, banks, and, most importantly, tech media companies. Anyone could have had a 50 percent interest for $500,000. Finally, Jim Mulholland, Jr., a 72-year old former tech media publisher, put up $1.2 million for one-third of the business. Jim made about $60 million on that investment in five years. But in 1993, when things started to really percolate around the Internet (before the World Wide Web was introduced), all the top tech media people turned down my offer. This included International Data Group (Pat McGovern, Pat Kenealy); ZiffDavis (Phillip Korsant, Scott Briggs, Eric Hippeau, Tom Thompson); CMP (Michael Leeds and Ken Cron); and Cowles Business Media (Herschel Sarbin). I chose the path of a public offering in February 1994, working with a tiny Denver, Colorado, investment bank, and raised $5 million, even though the "smart lawyers" told me I would fail. By late 1994 (and through 1996), IDG, ZiffDavis, CMP and others attempted to destroy Mecklermedia by throwing millions of dollars into creating new magazines and newspapers, as well as a variety of trade shows. Or they took existing, mammoth tech trade shows and added an Internet show within them. Every one of these attempts failed.

At any point from 1994 to 1996, if the "right" offer had been made, we most likely would have sold. Instead, all of these giants not only threw away millions, they sniped and started rumors about Meckermedia not being a real b2b company, or worse. They tried using their influence with marketers at IBM, Microsoft and others to get these behemoths to pull away from Mecklermedia events and publications.

This keeps happening, even today. Take my latest event, research company and website called Inside Quantum Technology. We were first to market. However, recently, a well-heeled English event company liked our idea so much that it started a competitive show, basically ripping off our brand and using almost the same design for their website! At this writing, I am at war with this English company because I believe this new field, quantum computing, will be immense. Perhaps both of us will do well? We shall see. But the nastiness of the other side, their attempts to destroy our assets, would be astounding had I not witnessed it all before, countless times over my career.

Getting back to the period 1994-1995, I have elsewhere related the threats Eric Hippeau made after I turned down his $30 million cash offer for my *Internet World* magazine. He basically gave me a "take it or leave it" ultimatum, and held up a dummy version of the Ziff Davis Internet magazine, which he said was on the drawing board. My net worth at the time consisted of a few million dollars of Mecklermedia stock, but I knew the combination of my magazine and the Internet World trade shows was strong. But this is where being paranoid is helpful. While feeling I had strength, I knew I had to be very wary and keep improving our products because giant media companies were gunning for me.

I learned to play hardball in my library tech publishing days, when the fraternity of similarly themed publishers was small and aggressive. Being such a publisher, there was usually only room in the research library budget to purchase one guide or one reference to a particular field. So being first to market increases one's chances of success immensely. Direct mail was the way to market in those days. I would send out 20,000 brochures and hope a few hundred libraries would order initially. If the publication was well reviewed, then success was assured. But again, I had to always be aware of a competitor going for a better product or putting out false claims to hurt my position.

Good ideas are not unique to one person. I had several wars with the likes of Jeff Pemberton (Vignette, "The Pemberton Lesson"), who seemed to be on my path many times. Jeff may have been first to see online delivery of information, but I was first with CD-ROM and Internet. Generally, he would launch something similar to me, almost at the same time. Then it became a fierce struggle to become "the" title, the one that the 3000 research libraries in the world would give allegiance to. Another incredible competitor from those days was Roger Bilboul in England, who partnered with Tom Hogan in the U.S. All of us had some nasty bouts. We are professionally friendly today, as I jumped to higher horizons and left the library tech field. However, from 1980 to 1993, I was tempered by the fire of my nasty fights and constant paranoia with these fellows. The lesson here is to have thick skin, be persistent, be able to adapt, and be aggressive. Most of all, be paranoid and think of what Mark Zuckerberg did to the Winklevoss twins, or what Bill Gates did to Steve Jobs, or what Steve Jobs did to Xerox. There are countless more examples.

BEING CURIOUS

I have written about awareness and paranoia as being necessities for the entrepreneur. Another important asset is curiosity. I realize that my whole adult life has revolved around being curious about almost everything. Having Google these days makes it easy to be curious, as one can almost immediately find an answer about an event, a fact, or an idea.

Some of my best (and worst) ideas have come about from being curious. For example, meeting a white-collar crime attorney at a cocktail party in the 1980s led me to start a newsletter for this community. I met the fellow at a back-to-school evening for one of my children in New York City. When he told me what he did for a living, my curious nature caused me to ask him if there was a publication that covered the field. When he said no, I immediately did some research and found that, in fact, there were no white-collar crime publications. (In those days, the only way to go was print, whereas today one can launch a website at a fraction of the cost.) I called my new acquaintance and asked for the names of others in the field, with the goal of creating an editorial board. Soon, I had about eight important New York City attorneys or professors at law schools as my editorial board. I was off to the races with another publication.

There is a saying, "curiosity killed the cat," and in my case, being curious led to creating too many publications. I could not turn down what I considered a good idea. By the late 1980s, I had 27 publications in a myriad of fields. Honestly, I think all of the titles were excellent. The problem was, I did not have the funding or cashflow to have continuous subscription promotion campaigns going, and so many of the titles suffered financially. Even today, I am always curious, from how a restaurant operates to how better to load airline passengers.

Being curious helps the entrepreneur to adapt. Being able to adapt helps one move on from difficult conditions or situations. Adapting and curiousness go hand in hand. If you have a competitor, being curious helps you analyze what the competitor might be doing better than you or helps you jump in front because you realize you have to adapt to survive.

Take the successful media entrepreneur Rafat Ali, who created a wonderful first business called PaidContent.org by being curious about why there was no blog reporting on the growing business of paid online content. After he sold that business, he grew curious about why the traditional business websites reporting on the travel industry were so pedestrian. Soon he had a plan and adapted. Next he raised funds, and now has a thriving business called Skift.com, which will one day sell for $100 million or more, I predict.

Or take James Dyson and his various electronic inventions. He revolutionized vacuum cleaners and other appliances because he was curious why the industry was pedestrian. Could he make something better? He did, many times over.

Throughout history curiosity has led to invention, and in the case of the entrepreneur, it has led to fortunes being made. Of course, being curious does not mean one can operate a business. However, one needs a great idea first in order to make a mark. And being curious is the first step to developing great business ideas.

DELEGATING

The entrepreneur needs to be aware and curious, and has to be able to multitask. Another asset is the ability to delegate responsibilities to staff or freelancers.

Over the years, I have observed startup entrepreneurs who find it very difficult to delegate as their business begins to grow. There is a fine line between doing the work yourself and spending too much money by hiring staff too quickly. This is a ticklish dilemma. Once funding starts to grow, or business starts to bring in significant revenue, it is easy to too rapidly add staff instead of multitasking yourself until you are overwhelmed.

During the go-go Internet years, I witnessed startups go under once funding dried up because they had staffed up too rapidly and had drugged themselves on the idea that there would always be more funding available. Recently, I came across a company in my VC portfolio in the blockchain space that seemed to be inundated with funding opportunities. But when the blockchain funding cooled down, the founders were suddenly choking on over hiring (and the correspondingly huge monthly burn rate). There is no perfect formula, other than an awareness that money in the bank is always the most important product for a startup and that one cannot count on funding being available forever.

Being able to delegate is a key asset for the entrepreneur. In my case, I am a great multitasker, but I was never able to work with a secretary. I am always amused when a secretary for an entrepreneur or even an executive at a prosperous company contacts me on behalf of his or her boss. This always seems like adding extra steps to the simple task of arranging for a meeting or lunch. This was true pre-Internet, and is even truer these days, with all the meeting apps and means of contacting an associate or business contact. One lesson I learned years ago was to never pick up a piece of paper that needed addressing and then placing it back on my desk or in a pile to be handled later.

"Pick it up and do it" has worked wonders for me. Delegating is one of my skills, but also has caused some disasters. The CFO, and later COO, I spent many years with, and who I daresay cost me hundreds of millions of dollars, became too much of a crutch for me. He worked incredible hours and never seemed to shirk from a task or a project. This became a drug to me, and in hindsight I should have handled some projects or overseen some meetings, rather than delegating them to this fellow. Don't get me wrong. This fellow had some great skills, but as the stakes got bigger, he was not up to handling the load and was too intent on protecting his turf instead of making sure the tasks were completed. This included keeping on as CFO a fellow who was way over his head as our stock photo business grew. These two fellows could never get the financial reporting in order, and the COO kept on a CTO who was overwhelmed as well. By that time in my career, I was over-delegating.

Delegating has served me well, but this management style caused a calamity. These days, as I write this book in 2020, I have a small business and delegate once again, mostly to my son who joined me full-time in 2016. The two of us, outside developers, six full-time employees, 10 freelancers, and no office is my empire these days.

But should things develop, I will be ready to bring in extra help. The lesson here is that one will do better as an entrepreneur if one can be aware, curious and able to delegate. These assets, with a dose of being a leader, is a winning combination when coupled with a great business idea.

EARLY BITCOIN MEMORIES

My Bitcoin and cryptocurrency startups followed a pattern and plan that I have used many times since the 1970s: find a topic, start a publication and a companion event, and perhaps add in other services.

The idea always is to build a community with information, and then sell other services. The plan is a good one, although it does not always work if the vertical premise behind the plan is a technology or topic that takes off for a short period, but then proves to be unsustainable, which can happen when the subject or field does not continue to evolve and grow. In order for the method to work, the topic (for example, Bitcoin) has to continue to develop, evolve and bring in investor interest. WiFi is a great example of a technology I jumped on in its infancy with a website and an event. It looked to be a big winner, with lots of promise. Yet within four years of launch, my enterprise crashed because WiFi technology, although still with us and very important, did not continue to change and evolve. It simply did not warrant annual events or daily news coverage.

This problem plagued some of my other launches too, such as those in nanotechnology and HDTV. However, my Bitcoin/cryptocurrency endeavors no longer exist mainly because I became ill from a deep vein thrombosis (DVT), or blood clot, and resulting emboli (several embolisms), which necessitated my being sidelined for almost two years, from 2015 to 2017, just as the blockchain revolution erupted.

I learned about Bitcoin from an employee named Ivan Raszl in the spring of 2013. We started our first event in the summer of 2013, and it was successful. The flaw at the time was that we weren't first to market in this fledgling industry, mediawise. There was already a news website called CoinDesk, published out of England by Shaq Khan, that had a big lead in readership over my startup, Inside Bitcoins. Shaq came to our first event in New York City and professed no interest in getting into events. I suggested that I would like to purchase his property, but he had no interest in selling. I smelled a great success and plunged into starting several Inside Bitcoins events. By 2015, I was producing events annually in New York, Las Vegas, Paris, Berlin, London, Hong Kong, Singapore and Melbourne. Our companion blog, Inside Bitcoins, was growing nicely, but was a distant second to CoinDesk. A few other competitor events existed in the field, but none threatened ours.

I came across some interesting characters during these Bitcoin years between 2013 and 2015, including the former child actor Brock Pierce, China's Bobby Lee, Chicago entrepreneur Matthew Roszak, and Perianne Boring, who now runs the Chamber of Digital Commerce in Washington, D.C. And then there was one of my developers at the time, Brandon Chez, who developed and owns a valuable industry website called CoinMarketCap.com.

Did Brandon get the idea while working for me? He was a mid-level developer at my company, but out of 75 employees he was the only person who knew the ins and outs of digital wallets and the nuances of the then-infant Bitcoin marketplace. As we ran our conferences, I soon found out who could be trusted and who could not. I remember running our New York City event at the Javits Convention Center in 2015 and chatting with Brock Pierce, only to find out he was behind a competitive event he was launching in New York. Brock is now a Bitcoin billionaire, according to the press.

Toward the end of 2015, I sensed that blockchain was going to be the star of the cryptocurrency field. As the enabling technology behind Bitcoin, it appealed to the financial community, including large banks and insurance companies, as well as the tech community, which was starting to conceptualize all sorts of nonfinancial applications for it, from healthcare records to real estate. Because of this, I started rebranding Inside Bitcoins as Blockchain Agenda, and planned to change the thrust of my shows.

I was still missing a large circulation news site. But a big break came when an associate of Shag Khan called me to dispose of the money-losing website.

This occurred in October 2015, and the offer was to sell the assets of the site to me for nothing more than to guarantee that I would take over payroll for the editors for a period of six months. I agreed to this deal, and was in the midst of completing it when I was struck down by the aforementioned DVT and had to bow out. About this time, a fellow named Ryan Selkis was putting together a new show for blockchain. Selkis was backed by Barry Silbert, who had, and continues to have, a number of investments in the cryptocurrency space. When I backed out of the CoinDesk deal, Selkis and Silbert took over CoinDesk, which in turn helped them create Consensus, which today is the No. 1 blockchain event in the world.

The basic gameplan of having a community, and then using it to build or sell other services, was perfectly executed by Selkis, with Silbert's financial backing. The irony of this history is that the current executive editor of CoinDesk is Marc Hochstein, who had the same position at the august American Banker. Marc had been working with me and my team, and had been a main cog in overseeing our Inside Bitcoins events. He had expressed interest in leaving American Banker to take over as editor-in-chief of Inside Bitcoins in late 2014. Marc ended up getting the CoinDesk gig after I bowed out. Another one of the key editors at CoinDesk, Pete Rizzo, several times chatted with me about jumping to Inside Bitcoins, but, alas, this did not come to pass as illness prevented me from executing what would have been another great tech media success.

I look back at these events and the interesting cast of characters I met producing Inside Bitcoins events around the world during the birth of the cryptocurrency industry. Although I missed out, at least I clearly saw what turned out to be a huge industry that will enjoy lots of upside for years to come.

A 30-MINUTE WINNER

Check out MDLinx.com. Back in 1999, two med students who were friends with one of my daughters asked to see me about creating an Internet startup. One evening, we met at my apartment in Manhattan. The two students, Evan and Rob, were at Columbia Medical School in New York City; their mentor was Mehmet Oz (who was not yet famous as television's Dr. Oz). I have now forgotten their idea, but while they were speaking, they sparked an idea for what became the very successful Mdlinx.com.

I suggested they use software that we were using at Internet.com. The software had been created by Rich Ord of Lexington, Kentucky, whose company we had acquired. Rich had several interesting products. For instance, he was one of the first people in those days to conceive of producing HTML-based email newsletters—an approach we used extensively. Rich also had created a simple product that could search the Web for any topic. In essence, it was a search bot.

After hearing out Evan and Rob, I suggested they consider using our software at no cost (Rich Ord's search bot) to seek out, every day, the best articles dealing with cardiology. Furthermore, the bot could break its cardiology findings into several vertical areas related to their field of interest, cardiology. As I saw them get excited, it also occurred to me that if the prototype worked, they could branch out into virtually every medical field. This way, their MDLinx.com could attract advertising from a variety of drug companies and services.

Since both Evan and Rob were full-time medical students, they needed to engage someone to handle the day-to-day aspects of building a startup, not to mention help them raise funds. One of their best friends from their undergrad days at Princeton was a fellow named Dave Rothenberg, who was looking to get involved in Internet startups. I interviewed Dave to be CEO, and my gut reaction was that he was a winner. The next step was raising funds. One of the first investors was Mehmet Oz, whom I met at a meeting at Evan's father's apartment in Manhattan. Oz was very animated and enthusiastic as I introduced him to the World Wide Web. Evan and Rob raised a few hundred thousand dollars, and Dave Rothenberg did the rest. Dave built a great team, based in Washington, D.C., and attracted a solid ad sales person. As I remember it, the biggest advertiser was Perdue Labs, maker of Oxycodone. I had no idea what this drug was, but noticed that ads for it were plastered all over the various medical verticals; as MDLinx grew by leaps and bounds, Perdue was soon spending hundreds of thousands of ad dollars.

I became a mentor to Dave and put him in touch with many of the Internet.com pros, who likewise passed on their knowledge. Soon, MDLinx was thriving. It was later sold to a Japanese company called M3, owned by Sony.

MDLinx is a good illustration of how I came up with ideas quickly in the course of a discussion, much as I had done my whole career. Fortunately, in this case, I did not try to make this an Internet.com product, but rather watched it thrive under the tutelage of Dave Rothenberg.

ENTREPRENEURS ARE A BREED APART

One of my current endeavors is overseeing Asimov Ventures. Asimov Ventures invests in early stage startups. Periodically, I attempt to raise funds from wealthy investors. I have learned that many of these people have inherited money and, for the most part, have a fundamental problem: they do not understand failure. Their money was handed to them, so they have a short fuse when it comes to hearing bad news about one of our portfolio investments. It is interesting to observe such reactions, particularly since I lived through 25 years of hearing mediocre or bad news about many of my startup ideas. In my case, I did not rely on outside investment, but somehow managed to struggle along with a few wins here and there, which fed a continuing string of new ideas that readily came into my mind.

When I started to try to raise money in 1992 for my idea that the Internet would be the "next great thing," I was met with ridicule and little understanding. Most of my potential investors were either people who inherited wealth or professional managers who dared not risk making an investment mistake. This latter group creates an environment that is fertile ground for startups and entrepreneurs, because professional managers are mistake-adverse, less they lose their jobs, and so tend not to want to invest in startups. They would rather pay through the nose for a startup that has *already* become successful, rather than invest in that startup's birth.

Entrepreneurs who create startups are a breed apart. They have dreams, and they have taken a lot of arrows in the back. James Grant of Grant's Interest Rate Observer recently wrote an article in *Barron's* that applies to entrepreneurs and, certainly, to my own experience. "Failure may or may not be good for the soul, but it's essential to a well rounded business education," Grant writes. He goes on to say this about the entrepreneur: "They know how to turn adversity into opportunity. Or they can summon the courage to try again when they really could go broke. They remember the people who stood by them, and they remember the ones who didn't."

When wearing my Asimov shoes and listening to entrepreneurs pitch their idea, I always put myself so easily into their shoes that I can hear their words as my words, my feelings, my worries and my salesmanship, and I'm often reminded what I endured in my efforts to raise funds or convince an established media company to invest in my businesses. Sometimes during these pitch meetings, I have to control my emotions so that I do not feel sorry for the pitcher. I have to hold back the urge to say to the entrepreneur, "I know you really need this money, and I am going to give you a chance because you are so earnest and I know you fear you will go broke." I hold back saying this because my experience, more often than not, tells me that the pitch is good, but the idea, in my opinion, cannot work. Many times during these meetings, I have thoughts running through my head, wondering if I am talking to the next Jack Ma, Jon Oringer, or even Jeff Pemberton. I have to fight off the urge to think that, whatever shred of viability every pitch contains, that it is, in fact, only a small shred and most likely will not work.

Fortunately, not every pitch I hear has someone behind it who gets into my head as a sincere person or one with whom I empathize. Besides, my two partners at Asimov Ventures can snap me back to reality if I "fall" for a pitched idea. The reality is, very few ideas will develop into any type of a winner. But in the end, on almost every pitch, whether it is in-person or on the telephone, at some point I identify with the pitcher. Memories of adversity, fear of failure, or going broke come into my mind for fleeting seconds. I admire anyone who gets into the arena of startups and entrepreneurship.

INTERNET SUCCESS
AND EMPLOYEE GROWTH

The early days of the commercial Internet at Mecklermedia were exhilarating. I had been a sort of ne'er-do-well for 20 years, with some interesting successes but nothing of a spectacular nature. All of a sudden, I had new hop in my step and every day proved to be exciting; I knew, and my small band of employees knew, that things were different. I went from not being sure I could make payroll every two weeks to watching money pour in for event registrations, booth sales and sponsorships. I had no idea that things would only get better. But to handle the growth, I had to have some super employees.

By 1994, Nancy Nelson and Tony Abbott had been with me for over a dozen years (in Tony's case, it was 19 years). Nancy, who grasped the Internet immediately, planned the program and Tony tackled everything editorial. Tony was a person of prodigious talents who could edit anything; Nancy could plan a conference in a week. They were both whizzes. Another interesting fellow was Paul Bonnington, who took over ad sales for the new *Internet World* magazine.

One day at work, I got a call out of the blue from Paul, who had experience selling advertising for tech magazines. He had bought a copy of *Internet World* on the newsstand and told me he noticed we lacked a director of sales. (In fact, the early issues had no advertising!) He lived in Norwalk, Connecticut, not too far from our Westport office, and asked if he could stop by. Paul arrived a few hours later with a comprehensive proposal of how to sell ad space for *Internet World* magazine. I loved his enthusiasm, and after checking out his references, he became director of ad sales a few days later. This was my gut decision-making at its best. Paul had contagious enthusiasm, even though some in the trade told me he could not lead a team. Within a year, we had a monthly magazine and a staff of four full-time sales people. Soon, we added *Web Developer* and *Internet Shopper* magazines, not to mention a weekly newspaper called *WebWeek*. Paul did a great job .

Another of my young turks was Paul Gudelis, who joined us from Ziff Davis. I also had a quirky young fellow named Tristan Louis, who understood tech and websites better than most and convinced me to change the name of our fledgling website from MecklerWeb to iWorld. Tristan at this time was way ahead of most people in the fledgling Internet space and helped get iWorld humming. Another part of the brain trust was a young writer named Andew Kantor. Still in his mid 20s, Andrew became one of our top writers, but he was also a deep thinker about where the Internet was headed.

As our stock took off, along with our trade show and magazine, the television powerhouse show *60 Minutes* contacted us, wanting to profile us in and around a story of how to search on the Web.

After scouting our office building, Lesley Stahl arrived with an army of aides. She used my office to videotape Andrew explaining to her how to use the Web and Internet. About this same time, I was the main guest on the PBS television show *Adam Smith's Money World*, where I made several predictions about the future of the Internet that have held up very well over 25 years. Another interesting fellow was our first full-time editor. I hired Mike Neubarth from obscurity, and Mike did great work for two years. But he was not the best communicator, and so we brought in Gus Venditto from Ziff Davis to take over as editor-in-chief.

Perhaps my wisest decision was selecting another rather obscure subeditor from CMP to become the founding editor of *WebWeek*. *Internet World*, being a monthly, had us losing out in print to the many computer weeklies from Ziff Davis, CMP and IDG. While they launched some lame competitors to *Internet World*, they each had a few weekly computer weeklies with Internet sections. I felt, and was correct, there was a need for a pure weekly covering enterprise Internet topics. I had noticed Rob's byline at CMP, and then, at Internet World San Jose in March 1995, I was standing on a food line and there was Rob immediately in front of me. Over the ten minutes it took to get to our place for food orders, I interviewed Rob and offered him the editor-in-chief job. He was incredulous! I told him I knew he could write, and felt in those few minutes he could also lead a team. Lo and behold, he called me the next day to say that his boss at CMP, Ken Cron, had told him that "one day" he could be an editor-in-chief, but that he needed more seasoning. Rob took this to heart, but all of the sudden he was a bit angry. He decided the time was right and the offer was great. He joined.

Rob was brilliant. A great leader. And two years later, when I decided to fold all of our magazines into a weekly called *Internet World* (changing the name of *Web Week* to *Internet World*, and stopping the monthly *Internet World*, as well as the bimonthlies *Web Developer* and *Internet Shopper*), I made Rob the editor-in-chief. I also moved Gus Venditto over to become editor-in-chief of our website iWORLD, which would soon become Internet. com.

It was about this time that we engaged Chris Elwell from Cowles Business Media as general manager in charge of ad sales for Internet.com. Chris, too, proved to be a great leader, and built a fabulous team. On the legal side, realizing we needed a house counsel, Mitch Eisenberg joined us. Mitch was a CPA and a trained attorney, with a business head, which proved valuable given our busy acquisition pace. We probably purchased 100 websites and related assets from the time we purchased The List — the first website acquisition in history — until we went public with Internet.com in 1999. As an aside, Mitch had worked for me part time from the time he was 10 years old (25 years earlier), when his mother worked for me during my library publishing days and would bring in her kids to stuff envelopes for pocket change.

A few other interesting people to mention are Ted Stevenson and Kevin Reichard, who came over from Ziff Davis. On the tech side, I was fortunate to have some great hires who stayed with me for years, such as Mark Berns, Peter Hegedus, Tom Kitt and a few more.

There were dozens of other wonderful workers who had great enthusiasm and who made great money from Mecklermedia stock options. There were some difficult times too, which, ironically, often had to do with stock options too. I once had to let a head of ad sales go after she tried to blackmail me over getting more stock options: either I triple her stock options or she was quitting. Soon she was on the street, looking for a job.

The lesson in all of this for the entrepreneur is to be able to pick talent "on the fly," but also to be willing to take a chance on a variety of young people and to get leads from current employees who can vouch for people they have worked with at other jobs.

In 1992, my privately held business was producing $2 million and losing over $200,000 annually with just 10 employees; I was using 20 credit cards to make ends meet. Less than three years later, revenues had exploded, we were an extremely profitable public company, we had 40 employees, and I could finally buy a new suit. It was a great ride that would only accelerate, but a major contributor to this success was finding the right team and being able to adapt and delegate.

The main trait I returned to over and over again was enthusiasm and understanding of the business. I had no interest in years of experience possessed by a candidate, as I had proven myself that a bit of experience, combined with a "can-do attitude" is a winning combination.

THE INTERNET FUND

Picture the year 1995 and the Internet. My company, Mecklermedia, had gone public in February 1994, and it was one of the few ways Wall Street could invest in the possibility that the Internet would become a commercial success.

Mecklermedia went public on February 11, 1994, at $6 a share on what was known as the "pink sheets," the home for companies not listed on major exchanges like the NYSE or the Nasdaq. Cohig, a Denver investment bank, handled the IPO. Within a few weeks of the public offer, public trading in the stock was so great that Mecklermedia (MECK) was listed on the Nasdaq. Even so, Mecklermedia was not widely known. But by October 1995, with the growth of our Internet World trade shows, the stock began obtaining a following. Nancy Peretsman of Allen and Company was the first significant Wall Street bank to realize that I was on to something big, and she wisely bonded with me. John Tinker of Montgomery Bank was another banker who saw the future and started visiting with me in Westport, Connecticut, to discuss the future of the Internet. I remember Tinker asking me about EBITDA and I had no knowledge of the term and had to move the conversation elsewhere.

By the end of 1995, I had been written about in Fortune and Forbes, and I had been on a few financial cable shows. I was in demand for breakfast meetings with a variety of investors and bankers.

One bank in particular that sought me out was the firm of Weiss, Peck and Greer. And from time to time I would be asked to give presentations to Wall Street banks, during which 30 to 50 bankers would show up to hear about the Internet and my views on its future. I remember Barry Fierstein having me as the keynoter at his annual hedge fund dinner.

This brings me to a morning meeting at the New York City office of Janney Montgomery Scott on Wall Street. As I remember it, it was early 1996. Some 50 staffers appeared for my 8 a.m. talk about the future of the Internet and, indirectly, Mecklermedia stock. I gave my standard talk, in which I mentioned my background, how I learned about the Internet, how I was turned down by investors when trying to raise funds and, of course, the success of our Internet World trade shows. Following the talk, I took questions. One of the questioners asked me the following: "What would you be doing now in the Internet space if you were not CEO of Mecklermedia?" My answer came rapidly because I had contemplated it for over a year: "I would start a mutual fund specifically to invest in the Internet." As the meeting broke up, the questioner, a Janney employee named Larry Doyle, came up and introduced himself. Larry probed a bit more about my response, asking again why I would start such a fund. "That the idea came to me several months ago, because I am constantly being asked what stocks one should consider buying if one wants to invest in the Internet," I told him. I knew the limited selection of publicly traded companies very well, as Mecklermedia had become the center of all things Internet. Besides, we were covering the space editorially on our iWorld website, and I was already reading the writings of Jupiter Research analyst Steve Harmon (who later joined Mecklermedia). So I saw the opportunity. "However," I told Larry, "it would be a conflict of interest for me to be involved with an Internet mutual fund while running Mecklermedia and overseeing editorial and conference coverage of Internet content and companies." Larry mulled this over, and I could see he did not necessarily agree with my viewpoint. He took my business card and suggested he would like to pursue the concept in a phone call or email. I did not expect to hear from him, but a short time later he called me, telling me that while he could not afford to give up his job, he was going to start a fund called the Internet Fund (my idea). "I hope you don't mind," he added, and then went on to offer me equity, wanting me to invest and/or consider being on his board. I was flattered but had to decline both invitations for the reasons already stated.

A few months later, Larry got in touch again and sent me a very modestly designed flyer announcing the formation of the Internet Fund, which listed his home or his mother's home address in North Babylon, Long Island, as the office of record for his new fund. His mother, as I remember it, was listed as president of the fund. In a strange way I was envious that he took my idea and launched a fund, but I felt that it was wonderful for Larry, and I was pleased to see my idea coming to fruition.

Later, Larry brought in his brother Peter to run the fund, and today both the Doyles are worth many millions off the backs of this fund, which still exists today as part of the Kinetics Mutual Funds family of funds.

The Internet Fund raised little money at first (about $12 million in 1996, its first year), but by 1999 it was managing close to $300 million, after providing a return of close to 200 percent in 1998. The Doyles sold the fund at one time for several hundred million; Peter Doyle is still active with Kinetics while his brother Larry is on the board and does other investing. Ironically, while I was first meeting with Larry, my Wall Street journeys and visits put me in touch with his sister Maura Doyle, an investment advisor at a boutique Wall Street firm. As I understand it, Maura made a bundle on Mecklermedia and several other Internet stocks and retired to make movies. I was never aware of the connection.

Looking back at my career, this is one of my favorite stories because it demonstrates my idea-creation abilities and because, in this case, the people who executed my idea made a lot of money. In my early years as a scholarly book and library tech publisher, I created dozens of important reference books and publications that helped me make a modest living. But the Internet was where I hit the jackpot personally and for many other people, including the Doyle family.

ON INTERNET

In 1993, with the help of Tony Abbott, I created a directory called *On Internet*. At the time, it was a logical extension of my primary business model: create a community via a print publication (later, websites), and then, once the publication gained an audience, start selling related services, such as databases, directories, research and conferences. I had used this model over and over again, and still use it today. Of course, it does not always work.

In the 1970s, I created the publication *Micorform Review*, and then started publishing guide books and database directories, and then started my first conference, Library Microform Conference, in 1975. In the early 1980s, I started a publication called *Optical Information Systems* and a trade show by the same name to cover the fledgling CD-ROM industry. In this same decade, I started an event for HDTV technology, in association with a publication owned by a fellow named Dale Cluff (that one did not work). Finally, I turned a newsletter called *Computers in Libraries*, which had been started by the University of Arizona Graduate Library School, into a magazine and a successful show by the same name, which I produced annually in England, Canada and the U.S. This publication spawned countless directories and guides for librarians and introduced me to the Internet. Interestingly, the U.S. event, now in its 35th year, continues with the company I sold it to in 1995.

But my most notable success was developing *Internet World*, first as a newsletter and then as a magazine, between 1993 and 1994. Because of the newsletter, and because, at first, I only foresaw the Internet being used by libraries and research organizations, the concept for *On Internet*, when Tony and I started working on the project, was a directory of every piece of information available on the fledgling Internet at that time. (Remember, back then, websites did not yet exist.)

We engaged several librarians as freelancers to collect information and to portray it by author, title and subject — much like a reference directory at the time called *Books In Print*, which was the Bible of bookstores and libraries for listing every known book in print. (In the end, the directory compiled several thousand resources that could be found on the fledgling Internet in the fall of 1993.)

Looking back, it is hard to believe we did not think of creating this product online. It would only be around 18 months later that Jerry Yang and David Filo came up with the same idea for Yahoo, which would be a similar directory to ours, but published online. I remember how excited Tony and I were about the prospects for this new directory, which we could tell was going to be our most successful project in an almost 20-year collaboration of creating directories and guides for the research community.

We timed the launch and publication of *On Internet* with the December 1993 Internet World trade show at the Javits Center in New York City. We priced the book at $35 and sold hundreds of copies at the show. More important were the thousands of direct mail sales of the directory, our greatest success ever for our company at the time. At this point in my career I had published more than 800 books of all types for libraries, and the best seller up to this point was probably in the neighborhood of 3,000 copies. *On Internet* sold about 30,000 copies! We rejoiced at this incredible critical and financial success. On the other hand, this success was really a failure. Tony and I did not have the background or total understanding yet about the upcoming World Wide Web, and so we missed the smart move of immediately placing the content online via a website open it to the world and to which we could add information at will. In hindsight, Tony and I had the makings of the first Internet search engine well before Yahoo. But we missed it while celebrating what was, for us, an incredible financial win with a book product, one that was overwhelmingly our best seller over a 20-year run.

As I look back over these years, I see a lot of "woulda, coulda, shoulda" decisions that I should have made, such as not investing in Alibaba, Shutterstock or a few other startups. Yet all of those decisions were ones in which I was not entirely in control of the situation. The *On Internet* miss, of missing out on being the first search engine on the Web, was totally controllable. But I was, at heart, a man of print and not of the Internet and the Web. Yes, I was the first person to create a commercial venture in the Internet space with *Internet World* the publication and conference, but I was not tech savvy, and I was too imbued with my book and periodical history.

I presume *On Internet* can still be found in the stacks of research libraries around the world. I no longer have a copy of the early *Internet World* magazine or newsletter, but for some reason I keep a copy of *On Internet* in my study. And for some reason, I think about the "what if," about the direction I chose for the product in 1993, more than any other decision in my career. I presume this condition exists because I have never shed my love of books and my first commercial efforts in the 1970s.

THE STRANGE CASE
OF AOL AND YAHOO

As one of the first, if not *the* first, people to start a commercial Internet venture in 1990, I have had an interesting perch from which to observe theories, trends and outcomes for 30 years in the Internet space. During the rise of America Online, I voiced many times my feeling that, as AOL rose to huge valuations, it had a flawed model.

At first, AOL was an easy method for one to send emails and view the World Wide Web. It was a mammoth internet service provider, but as a student of the industry, and as the owner of ISPCON (the trade show of record for the ISP industry), it became apparent to me that, one day, ISPs would be doomed. Fortunately, I sold Mecklermedia in 1998, before the decline in ISP values became more widely apparent.

It is amazing to me that the famous Mary Meeker, then of Morgan Stanley, continued to extol the virtues and values of AOL well into the 1990s. In fact, she was famous for proclaiming at one point that everyone else in the space was wasting their time taking on AOL. A well-known Bank of America analyst in the late 1990s named Alan Braverman was another who became famous for riding the coattails of AOL's stock price rise. And, of course, Time Warner believed all this hype. It did not understand the huge flaw in the AOL model, and went out and spent billions merging with AOL in early 2000, a few months before the crash of Internet valuations.

I saw that AOL had nothing unique in terms of content, and that its paid subscription model for connectivity was doomed. Steve Case, founder of AOL, was a master marketer who played selling AOL to the suckers at Time Warner perfectly. I remember Ted Turner saying that the AOL deal was "better than sex!" Meanwhile, the CEO of Time Warner, Jerry Levin, was fleeced. Having missed the rise of the Internet, he then realized that Time Warner was not a major player. So he went out and, in desperation, made (along with his board) one of the worst business deals in history. Every one of the board members, including Ted Turner, had ignored the rise and future of the Internet for many years and then, in an effort to make up for lost time, made the AOL deal.

I was incredulous to read this news in early January 2000. Fast forward and, amazingly, Verizon, run by a CEO who was overall clueless about content value and the value of AOL, did another disastrous deal, buying AOL a few years ago. (That $4.4 billion expense had to be written off.) The same CEO bought another mostly worthless property in Yahoo! Both properties had seen their better days, but boardroom decisions by directors and executives who did not understand the difference between "eyeballs" and "valuable eyeballs" wasted billions.

Speaking of Yahoo, that was another brand from the 1990s that was mishandled. Whereas AOL was masterfully marketed and made the founders billions, Yahoo was never marketed. Yahoo had great value with its first-move advantage as a search engine and portal, but the founders, and the management they engaged, ruined the headstart and valuation over a 20-year period. I had the pleasure of meeting the Yahoo founders Jerry Yang and David Filo at Internet World in Washington, D.C., in December 1994, when my team of Bill Washburn and Chris Locke got a handshake agreement for Yahoo to become featured on our MecklerWeb site (soon to be called iWORLD). Unfortunately, later on at the show, the Netscape team, headed by Jim Clark and Jim Barksdale, trumped our offer, and got Yahoo to park itself on the recently launched Netscape homepage. For Jerry and David, this was certainly the better choice, and Yahoo traffic and use surged along with Netscape's.

In the spring of 1995, I met with Jerry and David for dinner at Internet World San Jose to discuss Mecklermedia either buying Yahoo or taking a significant interest, in turn for a large, multimillion payment. This meeting had been arranged by Bill Washburn, who knew both fellows very well. It was at this meeting that I was told the VC firm Sequoia was the front runner for making an investment, and that Jerry and David (who was accompanied by his girlfriend) would make a decision on which way they would go the next day. They decided on Sequoia, and the history of their IPO, and the company's next few years, was a gigantic success, enriching all concerned.

Over the years, I never could understand how Jerry and David brought in such an unspectacular CEOs as Tim Koogle. Koogle was a clueless fellow. I used to say a chimpanzee could be the CEO of Yahoo and the company would still dominate. They later brought in Terry Semel, a Hollywood producer, who was equally clueless, but appeared brilliant because Yahoo was, at the time, the go-to search directory. Unfortunately for all, Semel decided not to buy Google after his excellent $1.63 billion purchase of search company Overture Services, which was essentially the decision that led to a slow decline in Yahoo's value and place in the Internet pantheon of great brands with longevity. (Buying Overture probably was the reason they did not buy Google.)

Jerry and David then brought in Marissa Mayer from Google to be CEO. This, too, was a strange hire, as Mayer's only background was as an early Google employee with great design sense. She got a lot of press by making some ridiculous acquisitions, such as the microblogging and social networking site Tumblr. Ultimately, Mayer was paid many millions to leave when the same CEO at Verizon who bought AOL also bought Yahoo. I presume he thought he had just conquered the Internet!

Today, Yahoo is an interesting brand, but no longer, except in Japan, of great value. Masayoshi Son made a large investment in Yahoo in the 1990s and got the rights to oversee it in Japan, where it still has importance.

I publicly suggested that Yahoo should have purchased Dow Jones when it was put up for sale, and then leveraged the once-important Yahoo Finance with the Dow Jones financial reporting assets, thereby giving it gravitas in financial content. Those who founded AOL and Yahoo made billions, so congratulations to them. AOL was always doomed, based on its business model and tertiary content holdings. Yahoo, on the other hand, could still be one of the great brands of the world, if not the greatest Internet brand in the world.

CITYBIKEBASKET

I have always been impressed that Abraham Lincoln was awarded a patent from the United States Patent Office. He received Patent No. 6469 in 1849, for a device to lift boats over shoals. Although Lincoln's lift was never manufactured, he is the only U.S. president to have a patent. I am pleased to have a patent for something too. Mine is called the CityBikeBasket.

As I have mentioned throughout this book, I have a "painful" kind of awareness that seems always to be with me. Back in 2014, when Citi Bikes started to appear in bike racks in New York City, I came up with an idea. It was simple, and as I thought about it, very necessary and even more practical. None of the bikes-for-hire had bike baskets, and I noticed that riders often thrust their gear into a metallic object in front of the handle bar, or carried things in one hand, or used a backpack. My idea was to invent and manufacture a plastic bike basket that would fit snugly onto and over the metal device on the front of the handlebars on these bikes. After much research, I came across a design engineer who, after five iterations, created a molded plastic bike basket that weighed in at about 2 pounds. It was designed with a detachable handle, so that the user could easily lift and carry the basket from home or office to the bike rack and then again to home. I engaged a top-flight patent attorney to go along with my designer. My prototypes were manufactured in Taiwan.

In 2018, I was ready to start selling the basket at www.citybikebasket. com, a website I'd created. I had spent $185,000 for the patent and the engineering, the prototypes, and a first order of 500 baskets. Sadly, the product did not go viral. I did some advertising and sent a basket to local newspapers in New York City, but at best I have sold, as of this writing, but 100 baskets. I even placed 300 on special Citi Bikes in Manhattan, but even this didn't result in many orders. I concluded that the average person who uses a Citi Bike in New York City travels with a backpack, or simply does not care if what they jam on top of the handlebar falls or gets caught up in the front wheel.

CityBikeBasket was one venture I could have done without. The endeavor was very much like my thrusts into new and unfocused publishing ventures back in the 1980s. Fortunately, I had the funds to take the plunge, but it was not focused on my main area of technology publishing and investing.

Interestingly, my web developer at the time, a fellow named Kevin Lane, was watching this project as he built the bike basket website. It inspired him to become an entrepreneur himself, and to develop plastic molds to make sand and snow castles. He used my design engineer, patent attorney, and public relations service. Kevin's product, Create A Castle, won toy product of the year at the 2020 toy trade show in New York City. He is now well on his way to making some great money. He demonstrated an awareness and drive that an entrepreneur needs to be successful.

Looking back, I am pleased to be a patent holder. It goes well with my Ph.D. in American history, and I am now a fellow, along with Abraham Lincoln, in the patent fraternity. (Although there are days when I can see how I could have better used that $185,000.)

INTERNET.COM

Mecklermedia went public on February 4, 1994. At the time, the company had three tech magazines: *Internet World, CD-ROM World* and *Virtual Reality World*. It also had one of the first websites in the world, Mecklerweb.com. This was a period when few if any Wall Street followers knew the term Internet, and fewer comprehended the term World Wide Web.

Mecklerweb was the brainchild of a fellow who worked for me named Chris Locke. Chris was one of the handful of people in the world at the time who could intelligently speak about websites and the future of the Internet. Another fellow who worked for me at the time was Bill Washburn, who had been involved in government work on the future of the Internet and had recently worked on a nonprofit Internet Service Provider project called KIX. These two were an incredible Internet brain trust for the recently-gone-public Mecklermedia. As word got out about Mecklermedia being one of the few ways "to play" the public market in the Internet space, I would get dozens of requests to be interviewed. Whenever possible, I had Chris or Bill nearby to answer technical questions (as I was still learning the ins and outs of this exciting new technology).

Chris remained with Mecklermedia for a few more months, but a falling out over the future of Mecklerweb forced me to terminate him. Bill remained for another 18 months. By the time Chris was out the door, I had hired a 23-year-old fellow named Tristan Louis to become my hands-on guru for all things Mecklerweb. With Tristan's help, we started to move Mecklerweb into a vertical portal to discuss all things related to the business of the Internet. We also used Mecklerweb to help promote the Internet World trade shows and our magazine of the same name. As we moved closer to the 1995 fall Internet World trade show at the World Trade Center in Boston, Tristan wisely convinced me to change the Mecklerweb name to iWorld.com, a URL he had come across. It was a good choice, and we continued our quest to load more and more information onto the website about Internet business and web development news. We launched the new design and name at the Boston event; both were well received by the press and the Internet community.

Tristan moved on about two years later, about the time Jeff Dearth arrived to oversee *Internet World* magazine and iWorld. One day, in the summer of 1997, Jeff and some of the tech team approached me to say that the entrepreneur who owned the URL Internet.com was having financial problems and wanted to sell the URL quickly. A brief conference call about our willingness to wire funds within 24 hours brought us the highly prized Internet.com URL for the price of $200,000.

The changeover from iWorld to Internet.com went smoothly. And when Mecklermedia was sold to Penton in the fall of 1998—I have related how Penton was terrified of the finances of a website and its potentially adverse effect on its public company finances—a deal was struck simultaneously with the sale, made me the owner of Internet.com and its related assets for a price of $18 million. By June 1999, I was able to go public once again as Internet.com, at $14 a share. Elsewhere I have taken readers through the IPO launch and the over $1 billion valuation that Internet.com achieved after a secondary offering in January 2000.

Ultimately, the Internet.com brand and related website assets were sold to the public company Quinstreet.com in 2010 for about $20 million in cash, thus ending the saga of my involvement with the brand. Quinstreet continues to own and use the URL, but the URL is no longer a news and web development portal. Ironically, iWorld.com is still owned by my current company, and I have related how Steve Jobs inquired about purchasing the URL in 2005. I still think it would be a natural for Apple, but since Steve Jobs passed away I have not heard from Tim Cook or anyone from Cupertino. Hardly a month goes by, however, without some individual or company contacting me about purchasing this URL. I feel it is worth at least the $500,000 Steve Jobs offered, so I am holding onto it.

MUTUAL FUND FORAY

My involvement with public financial vehicles has included two IPOs, in 2004 and 1999, three secondaries or follow-on offerings, in 1995, 2000, and 2004, and a foray into a stock mutual fund in 2014.

Launching a mutual fund is relatively easy compared to the preparation and roadshow work required for a public stock offering. The main difference is that a launch of a mutual fund does not involve outside investors; plus, no roadshow is needed. The cumbersome part of a mutual fund launch is dealing with the SEC, but since there are no historic financials, even dealing with the SEC is easy because there are no numbers that need vetting by the government. Besides needing a good and justifiable idea for the mutual fund, one needs a sophisticated law firm for representation.

My fund idea was simple and seemed like a great, money-making idea when I thought it up in the summer of 2013. I have mentioned how I became deeply involved in the field of additive manufacturing, better known as 3D printing. I had launched several trade shows in this field and had become invested in one of the larger B2B websites. By this time, several companies in the field had had successful public company launches, and much like my idea for a mutual fund to cover the field of Internet stocks in 1995, I noticed too that the 3D printing field had no fund that offered investors a way to invest in the rapid growing field. Of particular note were the roaringly successful public companies that had stock prices close to $100-a-share and which were, at that time, financial stars. Also, several companies were public in Germany and Sweden, so the field was exciting and ripe for a mutual fund launch. The cost to cover such a launch was at least $600,000, but I had the funds. In addition, I had a great wingman who knew the field and was a whiz with numbers and administration.

I settled on an international law firm to lead me through the process and the launch. A very experienced and seemingly straightforward partner took me under her wing and promised me an efficient and rapid path to a public launch in early 2014.

Another expense was the attorney at the SEC assigned to vet our prospectus. This bureaucrat was very leery that investors would throw money at a "red herring" fund in the sexy field of 3D printing. He continuously made us change language to try to fend off excessive excitement about the fund. In addition, we were calling my new baby 3D Printing Fund. This name was not satisfactory for the SEC. Our SEC overseer fought us tooth and nail that using this simple branding was tantamount to fleecing investors because the brand was, to quote him, "too exciting." Ultimately, his supervisor attended several conference calls for discussion about our desire to use the name 3D Printing Fund.

At first, all went well and money came in rapidly. In the month of February, my fund had a return of 5% or so, making it one of the best-performing technology mutual funds in the U.S. Then bad luck struck. Both high flyers stocks from Stratasys and 3D Systems reported disappointing earnings for their respective first quarters of 2014, and both stocks tumbled. This was an early death knell for the fund, much like the Internet crash of April 2000. The results caused a 3D printing stock crash in April 2014. And, of course, investors no longer saw the field as a way to make fast money, and investors no longer wanted to support the fund. Having had many highs and lows, I found myself fighting investment opinion. Ultimately, after another year, I was forced to shut down the 3D Printing and Technology Fund.

The mutual fund foray was yet another adventure. Everything pointed to a big win and financial success. But it was not to be. And as I write this book in 2021, while the 3D printing field is growing at over 20 percent a year, and Stratasys and 3D Systems have once again become profitable.

MANAGING MILLENNIALS

In over 50 years of running smaller- to medium-sized media companies and making VC investments, I have felt I was better than most in managing personnel. I have probably had 5,000 people working for me in offices, or as freelancers, or online. I am always aware of people's feelings and have, I believe, gone out of my way to think of those emotions in handling everything from the mundane, to the financial, to the personal. I only spent two years working for others, and in this brief period of time I saw how superiors treated people. I was shocked many times by superiors who were nasty or kind. Most of all, I knew that empathy was most important. How would I feel, or how would the other person feel, when a superior acted in certain ways (good or bad)? I have already mentioned that I played on many school and university sports teams, some of which involved as many as 30 teammates. Getting along with teammates on the field or in the locker room is good training. It was also good to watch how coaches handled difficult players or situations. But the best of all training was during my basic training in the Air Force, when I was placed in charge of 40 young men and having to interact with the drill sergeant and officers every day for six weeks. This continued with six years of two-week summer training camps in Air Force and Army Reserves, where, as an enlisted man, one came face to face with so-called weekend warriors: officers or noncommissioned officers who could throw their weight around once they were in uniform and in a military environment for short periods of time.

When it came time for me to hire my first employees, I was well-trained, and was always aware of their feelings. I would admonish anyone who showed disrespect and was ready to praise for the slightest good act or deed.

However, a lot of my feelings changed once I got involved in managing or dealing with millennials. The period between 2007 and 2012 was the most difficult time I had, personnel-wise, because I was mostly dealing with millennials. During this period, I owned the company Mediabistro in New York City, which was staffed almost entirely by millennials. And once Mediabistro got into purchasing and staffing acquisitions in the social media space, starting in 2009, the flood of millennials increased dramatically. Elsewhere I have written about a horrible time I had with the acquisition of Inside Social Media, which we purchased in 2011. Its writing staff knew no good manners, and was snotty, arrogant and incredibly self-entitled.

Today, as I write this book, I mostly deal with millennials in my venture capital doings. I have found many serious entrepreneurs, but in some cases, since money has been greatly available to startups in the period from just after the Great Recession to the pandemic of 2020, the attitude is often they are doing me a favor to listen to me and my advice once the initial funding has taken place. And much like the entrepreneurs before the Internet crash of 2000, millennial entrepreneurs at today's startups have the same attitude: the next round of investment will always be there for the taking. Perhaps this is because they have never witnessed a downturn in the flow of money since the Great Recession. Ten years of money flowing was a disease, and now there is a reckoning. My warning has always been, "Money in the bank is your most important product and concern." This is easily forgotten in good times and seems to be a curse in any era. Interestingly, my media properties these days have no dealings with millennials in terms of staff or freelancers. This is a relief for sure.

PREDICTIONS/
CONCLUSIONS

VISIONARY PREDICTIONS FROM 2000

The September 26, 2000 issue of *Business 2.0* magazine featured a story headlined "25 Visions of What's Next" commemorating 30 years since the publication of Alvin Toffler's landmark book, *Future Shock*. I was one of the 25 visionaries in the article, along with Bill Gates and Ray Kurzweil. The editors of the magazine entitled my vision "I Want My N/ TV," as my main projection was how the Internet would become a main competitor to conventional cable and television.

Twenty years later, many of my predictions have come to pass. I wrote: "There are a half-dozen major ways the Internet will change the media industry. . . . Magazines—both business and consumer—will find it hard to survive in the years ahead; only the strongest titles in a category will survive." On the subject of newspapers, I wrote this: "The Internet will drive down newspaper revenues as well. Daily and weekly newspapers that depend on classified advertising will find it impossible to keep up with Websites that can continuously update job listings."

YouTube and other similar services were not yet born in 2000, but I surmised their coming when I opined: "The big news of the next few years will be the creation of Net superstars and NetTV programs that seem to come out of nowhere ... professionals and entrepreneurs will move into this area by finding talent on the Web and creating of hundreds of NewBroadcast networks to rival ABC, CBS, NBC and Fox. These new Web networks will develop hand-in-glove with the growth of bandwidth."

I got one item wrong when I admonished *The Wall Street Journal* for having a paywall early on, saying that I felt its owners should have kept the site free to build massive readership, which could lead to many additional services that could be sold to this massive traffic. Time has proven that paywalls can work, as witnessed by the success of the *Journal*, along with that of *The New York Times* and many other media properties.

The most salient point about 2000 and what has happened in the past 20 years is the opportunities that were lost by many then-strong media companies, who had chief executives and managers who hung on too long to traditional methods of providing information, and so missed out by not throwing in with the revolution on delivering information. It was not unlike my experience with many potential investors in the early 1990s, when I attempted to raise funds for Internet World but found that media executives could not comprehend that the Internet was about to bring a wave of creative destruction—a phenomenon that continues to this day.

CONCLUSION

To be valuable, a memoir should be informative, interesting, poignant, heartfelt and reflective, so that a reader can identify in some fashion with the memoirist and, if fortunate, learn lessons and gain wisdom from the writer's memories.

I believe I have touched all of these points. I have been fortunate to have had a rich history, one that has brought me in contact with many fascinating people. Most of my contacts have been in the media-technology space, but I have also crossed paths with some world-class luminaries such as Robert F. Kennedy.

I have also been on the cutting edge of many technology developments, even though I am not technically proficient. Somehow, I am blessed with gifts that help me grasp the future of technology trends years before others see the light. However, I am equally flawed. I have made many wrong decisions by being too generous and loyal, and by not having the killer instinct that other great entrepreneurs possess. In fact, I have probably made more incorrect decisions than correct ones. Fortunately, being one of the first people to comprehend the commercial Internet outweighed my collection of poor decisions.

Looking back on my 50-year entrepreneurial journey, I see several themes that appear over and over again. I also see traits and characteristics that make a great and true entrepreneur.

No matter what one plans or hopes to accomplish as an entrepreneur, luck is the most important variable. While I believe hard work helps one garner luck, luck by itself cannot be planned. Unfortunately, when things do not work out, even after hard work, it is easy for some to blame their misfortune and failure on "bad" luck. The truth is, a great victory is often accompanied by lucky decision-making or a fortuitous event. Even the decision to take a "left or right fork" in the road, in terms of a business decision, can prove successful or not because of luck. Good luck is therefore probably the most important factor to being a successful entrepreneur.

The next necessary element of success is being blessed with certain traits. One can desire to be a successful entrepreneur, but without these attributes, it is hard to be one. In my case, I was the son of an entrepreneur who was a trailblazer in the vehicle leasing field. My father's career took off like a rocket, and he had for a time a huge net worth before crashing into bankruptcy. Still, I must have inherited a genetic propensity for entrepreneurism from him. My father was much smarter than I was, or ever will be, but he was done in by a major bad business decision at the height of his career, as well as the actions of an evil genius fraudster who caused his bankruptcy. Dad's rise, and particularly his fall, is worthy of a book.

My father was at the center of a master Ponzi scheme created by Jack Dick, who duped bankers, attorneys, accountants and hundreds of investors into believing that his tax shelter, Black Watch Farms, was a legitimate enterprise. My father purchased this business in the late 1960s through his public company, Bermec Leasing. Within one year of the acquisition, the fraud was revealed and my father was forced to declare bankruptcy. Jack Dick died mysteriously before going to jail, but it became increasingly clear that Dick was a master swindler with a unique approach to fooling sophisticated financiers.

My father was dynamic and thought, as they say, "outside the box." I, too, have been called dynamic, and clearly think outside the box. Fortunately, I have not faced bankruptcy, but I certainly missed some great opportunities to stay a billionaire along my entrepreneurial trek. So it certainly helps to have been born with a genetic makeup that leads to being an entrepreneur. Without such DNA, it is doubtful that one would ever think of giving entrepreneurism a try. Moving in this direction is equivalent to being hungry or breathing. It is just present, and one feels it at an early age.

If you have such a bent, this book will, no doubt, provide lessons and wisdom from 50 years of nonstop entrepreneurial effort. Supposing you have the genetic make-up, what else is needed to make a go of it? Where do ideas come from? Awareness and a wide-ranging interest in many fields is probably paramount to coming up with new ideas. I have related how every day I feel bombarded with ideas and concepts from my reading, watching or just walking down a street. It is almost burdensome to have these feelings, as it thrusts me into profound thoughts beyond business ideas and into the body politic and world affairs. Maybe I am a frustrated politician, from my two years working in Robert Kennedy's office, who channeled himself into being an entrepreneur. Awareness and having many interests, mixed with the right DNA, is the brew that makes one an entrepreneur.

If one has this aforementioned formula, there are several other characteristics and traits that are essential. Being adaptable is of the utmost importance. If one cannot adapt, if one is not willing to change rapidly, then one is doomed as an entrepreneur. This relates to being able to give up on an original plan, or changing it, or even walking away from the original concept and starting over again. Adaptability is also being able to work with a variety of people, and realizing that you will always come across individuals you do not like or even detest, but that, within reason, you have to be political and work with such people if they, at the time, have skills or services that can help you move along your project or fledgling business. I am not suggesting that one should bend to working with an immoral person, but being able to handle different personalities is important.

Most reading this book will not get the benefit of the military experience I had. But many will have been on a sports team or worked on team projects in school, where lessons can be gained in adapting to personalities in order to achieve group goals. I was fortunate to have an incredible and life-changing military experience without having to face danger. This was a rare blessing that I hold highly in my life experiences. Every day in a startup probably calls for some adaptability, so embrace the need to make this part of your everyday thoughts.

Resiliency cannot be emphasized too strongly. Setbacks and disappointments are part of every life. The entrepreneur, however, not only has life's daily existence setbacks or ups and downs, but also is going to see these compounded by mixing daily life hurdles with entrepreneurial hurdles. It is the rare entrepreneur who only sees success. Success is littered, most likely, with a multitude of disappointments. These disappointments can cause depression. In my case, I had many critical successes for 25 years, but no financial success. I had bouts of depression on many days and nights. Some setbacks were downright shocking and mentally crippling. But, somehow, I had a native resilience that kicked in, and the dark periods never lasted more than a day or two. This was very tough on my wife, who would hear me optimistically speak about a potential angel investor as a sure supporter, only to find out a few days later that my idea(s) had been rejected.

Resiliency is tied to being an optimist, or as the saying goes, "Seeing the glass half-filled instead of half-empty." In my 25 years of building up to my success with Internet World, I never lost my optimism but for a day here and there. That's not bad, considering that I must have had at least 50 instances of outright rejection for funding and another 50 concepts that I thought were winners that ended being, at best, break even or duds. In a way, I am like Dr. Pangloss from *Candide*. But if one wants to try being an entrepreneur, one must have a bit of "Panglossian" philosophy or pixie dust in order to persevere. The pain of short-term defeat can be almost unbearable, but having resilience and optimism overcomes the gloom.

The final lessons that I take from 50 years of being an entrepreneur is to meld all of the above with an understanding about teamwork, about being able to work with others in delegating and multitasking. All too often, I have witnessed competitors and startups where I have been an investor fail because the founder or founders simply cannot work with others or create an environment that makes underlings feel appreciated. Certainly, the main reason for this failure is not having empathy for others and their feelings. But these failures also point to not being able to delegate and multitask. Elon Musk and Jeff Bezos are brilliant, but beyond their drive, they each have had to work with others. Moreover, both men are able to multitask at the beginning of an endeavor and then delegate later to ensure growth. There are very few Musks or Bezos, but even a small enterprise cannot be successful without these traits being part of the founder.

As I finish this book, I am in the midst of perhaps one more attempt at being a successful entrepreneur. I've launched a website and matching event and research business called Inside Quantum Technology. At this date,

I am at the 20 month mark. My team consists of a handful of dedicated people. None are highly paid, but the whole team feels that we might very well be creating an important tech media company, and a brand, that will be well known around the world, much like the beginnings of the commercial Internet. Like my previous efforts, I have enlisted the help of a subject expert, someone who intimately knows the field and is able to make the endeavor unique. You'll see that I am employing every lesson above, and using my skills to make Inside Quantum Technology a critical and financial success. *I am optimistic. I am weathering some setbacks. I am adapting. I am multitasking. I am delegating.*

The jury is out. In another 12 months, I will know if, once again, my optimism and gut feelings have delivered a critical and financial success. Stay tuned.

INDEX

A

B

Marcus, Drew, 87
Mariano, Sargent David, 24, 25
Markoff, John, 9, 192
Mashable, 126, 139, 141
Mason, Harold, 20
Maxwell, Robert, 77–78
Mayer, Marissa, 257
McCormick Center, 105
McCullough, Brian, 195
McGovern, Pat, 49, 69–70, 103, 107, 197, 231
MCI, 101
McNey, Joe, 57
MDLinx.com, 241–242
Meadow Lane, 211–213
Mecklermedia, 3, 8, 27, 48, 49, 50, 132
Meckler Publishing, 51
MecklerWeb.com, 8, 54, 260
Mediabistro, 125–128, 140, 158–159, 265
Meeker, Mary, 94, 255
Meer, Johnny Vander, 230
Merrill Lynch, 215, 217
Microfiche, 20
Microfilm, 20, 164
Microform Review, Inc., 13, 22, 77, 145, 252
Microsoft, 105, 172, 196
Milberg Weiss, 59, 60, 92
Military background, 19, 23–25, 273
Military history, interest in, 199
Millennials, 264–265
Monnington, Steve, 13
Monolovicci, Gerry, 85
Montauk, 211–212
Mostel, Zero, 116
Mulholland Sr., Jim, 51, 69, 103, 138, 231
Multitasking, 227—228
Musk, Elon, 206, 274
mutual funds, 56–58, 262–263

P

Pacific Growth, 62, 65
PaidContent, 79, 235
Paid search, 64, 203–204
Paley, William, 87
Panglossian philosophy, 274
Paranoia, 10, 11, 231–233
Paris, Judith, 171
Patricof, Alan, 108
Pemberton, Jeff, 152, 233, 244
Pemberton lesson, 152–153, 233
Penton Media, 49, 92, 132, 261
Pepsi ice popsicles, 7
Peretsman, Nancy, 48, 49, 50, 85, 103, 249
Philosophy, business, 145–146
Photos.com, 121, 122, 123, 216
Pierce, Brock, 239
Piper Jaffray, 45, 62, 64
Plank, Marietta, 188
PLUMB, 90
Port Washington, New York, 19
Predictions, 269–270
Price, Jon, 100
Private client banks, 45–47

Q

Quantum computing, 202
Quantum Technology, 274
Quinstreet, 159, 261
Quint, Sam, 199

R

Raising funds, 171–172, 173, 174–175, 176–177
Ranch bet, making a, 173
Raszl, Ivan, 238
Ratschy, Sara, 64
Real estate, success with, 211–213
Real Networks, 106
Real Real, 218
Rebel Artist, 122, 123, 216
Recession, 214–217

U

Uben, Jeff, 82
UBM, 49, 50
United Business Media, 49, 179
United States Department of Agriculture, 220

V

VA Linux, 137–138
Vallee, Rudy, 116
Vargas, Patty, 123
Veaner, Allen, 21
Venditto, Gus, 246, 247
Verizon, 256
Vermeer Technologies, 190–191
VerticalNet, 63
Vietnam War, 23
Virtual reality, 193–194
Virtual Reality: Theory, Practice & Promise, 192
Virtual Reality World, 69, 193
Visonary predictions, 269–270

W

Wall Street players, 85–86
Walsh, John, 166
Washburn, Bill, 256, 260
Web Developer, 225, 226, 246, 247
Web Week, 246, 247
Weil Gotschal, 52
Wharton School, 75
White-Collar Crime Reporter, 162
Wife, 35, 36
WiFi Planet, 151
Williamhouse-Regency, 20
Willoughby, Jack, 130, 132
Wolff, Michael, 108, 179
World wide web, 9–10
Wynn, Early, 230

Y

Yahoo, 54, 64, 84, 105, 109, 253, 256–257
Yang, Jerry, 54, 105, 191, 253, 256–257

Yee, Min, 171, 172

Z
Zander, Ed, 105
Ziff, William, 180
Ziff Davis, 54, 102, 108, 174, 231
Zuckerberg, Mark, 194
Zynga, 140